ride fit

RIDE TO GET FIT AND STAY FIT

DAVID FIEDLER

BARRON'S

ridefit

RIDE TO GET FIT AND STAY FIT

DAVID FIEDLER

BARRON'S

This edition for the United States, its territories and dependencies, and Canada published in 2010 by Barron's Educational Series, Inc.

Conceived and created by
Axis Publishing Limited
8c Accommodation Road
London NW11 8ED
www.axispublishing.co.uk

Creative Director: Siän Keogh
Designer: Sean Keogh
Project Editor: Anna Southgate
Production: Bili Books

All inquiries should be addressed to:
Barron's Educational Series, Inc.
250 Wireless Blvd.
Hauppauge, NY 11788
www.barronseduc.com

Library of Congress Control Number:
2010928095

ISBN 13: 978-0-7641-4542-1
ISBN 10: 0-7641-4542-8

Printed in China
9 8 7 6 5 4 3 2 1

contents

introduction

Like many people, I learned to ride a bike during my grade school years. A bike at that time meant independence and freedom from having to rely on mom and dad to take me where I wanted to go. In early adolescence, the bike gave me the ability to go new places with my friends, explore areas we had never been and travel much farther than we could ever go just using our feet.

But then came age 16, and the driver's license. The car was suddenly everything, and the bike was pushed to the corner of the garage, neglected and dusty. Through college and early working years, the bike rarely came out, and certainly didn't seem to me to be a particularly practical nor desirable form of transportation.

But then came sort of an awakening: sometimes having to drive a car can be a real drag. Sitting in traffic. Finding a place to park. Paying for gas. I started to think a bit, and the bike suddenly became a practical alternative to getting around again. Plus it made me feel good and I lost weight. And in this age of environmental awareness, it was cool too because it's "green". But most importantly, it was a lot of fun.

Of course, you don't have to trade in your car to ride a bike. Many people ride solely for recreation and exercise and that in itself is terrific. It's enjoying the outdoors and time with friends and family in the best way I can imagine, and for all the same reasons that it was great as a kid: going new places on your own and exploring new areas—all under your own power.

And you can find the same benefits, too, from bicycling. It's affordable and available to everyone, regardless of your current level of fitness or experience. I may be biased, but as far as I'm concerned, biking is great, for all the reasons mentioned above and more. Everyone should ride a bike—as often as they can and as fast (or slow) as they'd like.

WHEELS OF TIME: A BRIEF HISTORY OF CYCLING

1418	Giovanni Fontana builds perhaps the first human-powered vehicle. It had four-wheels and a rope 'chain'.
1817	Karl Drais invents the dandy horse in Germany. Though it had two wheels and looked much like a bicycle, it had no pedals and had to be propelled by pushing off on the ground with the feet, much like a scooter.
1860s	The velocipede, the first bicycle with pedals, appears. The pedals were attached directly to the front wheel, and the "tires" were steel sheets much like a cart wheel.
1870s	The term "bicycle" is first used to describe the new version that is now better known as a high-wheeler.
1879	Englishman Henry Lawson patents a rear-wheel, chain-driven "safety" bicycle.
1884	**April 22** Carrying a spare shirt, some socks, and a rain coat that also served as his tent and bedroll, Thomas Stevens leaves San Francisco on the first transcontinental bicycle ride. He arrived in Boston on August 4. After crossing the ocean on a steamer, Stevens continued east through Europe and Asia, until he had completed the first around-the-world bike ride, finally returning to San Francisco in January 1886.
1903	The first Tour de France takes place. It was won by Maurice Garin, a 32-year-old, Italian-born chimney sweep.
1958	Women are allowed to compete in the world championships for the first time.
1995	Dutch cyclist Fred Rompelberg sets an absolute speed world cycling record of 167 miles per hour, drafting behind a dragster on the salt flats in Utah.
1999	Lance Armstrong wins the first of his seven (so far) Tours de France.
2009	After almost four years of retirement, Lance Armstrong returns to the Tour de France once more. He finished third overall.

getting things rolling

Do you know what sort of cyclist you want to be? Does it even matter? Whether you have the answers or not, you won't want to skip this chapter. Over the next few pages you'll find out how to get the very most out of this book, what you might want to consider before you start riding, how to set good goals that are right for you, and even how you might fit it all into your hectic everyday life.

the different types of cycling

From Lance Armstrong rocketing up a mountain in the Tour de France to the teenager launching himself off a plywood ramp and even the little old lady riding back from the store with her purchases, cycling is an activity that encompasses a surprising range of different ambitions, attitudes, and levels of fitness. Which one you choose is entirely up to you, but here's a quick overview of what to expect from some of the main types of cycling:

Road cycling

Essentially this is all about going as fast as possible, whether in a classic bunch race, (such as the Tour de France where most of the riders stick together for the major part of the race, then sprint for the finish), alone in a time-trial, or in one of the many organized century events that have grown in popularity over the past twenty years.
Dress code: Lycra, suntans, and very expensive racing bicycles.

Mountain biking

Mountain bikes are still the biggest selling type of bicycle, despite the fact that most of them never actually go off-road. True mountain biking is about riding trails through the woods, on dirt, gravel or sand, with obstacles like water, logs, and rocks to negotiate along the way.
Dress code: Durable, rugged shorts and longer-sleeved shirts, an adventurous spirit and—almost inevitably—mud.

BMX

Whether it's 360 tail-whips in a half-pipe, flying around a string of dirt jumps or grinding down a railing outside an office building, BMX riding is all about trying new tricks—the harder the better, and being unafraid of falling off the bike is a requirement.
Dress code: T-shirts and jeans, body armor like shin guards and such, plus a youthful sense of indestructibility.

REASONS TO RIDE

1 Regular exercise leads to stronger muscles and a more efficient heart and lungs.

2 As little as half an hour of cycling three or four times a week can help prevent various illnesses, from Type 2 diabetes to cancer.

3 Exercise releases natural "feel-good" chemicals that can help you combat stress and depression.

4 Some studies have even linked exercise with a sharper mind, a higher sex drive, and even slowing the aging process.

Cycling is a low-impact form of exercise, so it's easier on the joints and tendons than, say, running or team sports. That makes it an ideal form of exercise for almost everybody.

Touring

Perhaps the most relaxed form of cycling (touring events often have a maximum permitted top speed), touring's challenge comes from the massive distances that can be covered.
Dress code: Pretty much whatever feels comfortable.

Track

If you feel a real need for speed, look no further than the velodrome. Track races are fast, tactical, and very, very hard. Add in special bikes and the banked track and this is probably not the best place for the total novice to get started.
Dress code: Tight fitting Lycra uniforms and nerves of steel.

WHAT ABOUT 'JUST RIDING ALONG'?

It may seem that all the examples given here are a little competitive. But of course, you don't have to enter races to be a cyclist. Those clear-cut categories are just easiest to define. Much of the best riding you'll find is in casual trips around town: to the park with family or a friend, or taking your bike out to run errands. Any of these activities also offer the benefit of simple exercise and are a delight in their own right.

how to use this book

The five chapters of this book are written with one aim in mind: to give you a better understanding of how to use cycling to improve your health, enhance your quality of life, and above all have fun.

In **Chapter One** you've already discovered some of the different types of cycling, and learned what regular exercise can do for you. In the remaining few pages we'll also look at assessing your current fitness, what to do about learning (or relearning) to ride a bike, and finding motivation and ways to fit cycling comfortably into everyday life.

Chapter Two is all about equipment. We'll look at the different parts of a bike and give you some tips on what to buy and how to ensure that your bike fits correctly. We'll talk about helmets and other essential cycling accessories, and make some suggestions about what to wear on the bike in every season of the year.

Chapter Three focuses on skills and fitness. In it you'll find tutorials covering some of the basic necessities for safe cycling like braking and changing gears as well as more advanced techniques that you might find fun and useful. You'll also find a series of "off-the-bike" exercises that are certainly worthwhile to help your body recover after a ride as well as to improve your overall health and strength both on and off the bike.

Chapter Four, the final chapter of the book, contains a series of training programs organized into six levels. Each program is carefully created to improve your cycling fitness and help you achieve a specific goal, whether that's simply getting back into regular cycling or taking on a century ride—100 miles—in a single day. You can follow them in sequence, stepping up as you gradually grow more fit, or select the one that suits your current level and start working at that.

We won't be able to dig as deep into some topics as you might like, which is why you'll find some suggestions for further reading for each chapter at the very back of the book.

WHICH PROGRAM TO CHOOSE?

1 STARTER LEVEL 1
If you're new to cycling or regular exercise in general, start here and let us get you gently up to speed.

2 STARTER LEVEL 2
Assuming you can ride continuously for up to an hour, you can use this program to build your fitness in preparation for some longer rides.

3 INTERMEDIATE LEVEL 3
A plan to build you up to a three-hour long ride on the weekend.

4 INTERMEDIATE LEVEL 4
This twelve-week plan introduces some longer rides combined with shorter, more high-intensity efforts to develop your overall strength and speed.

5 EXPERT LEVEL 5
Believe it or not, riding 100 miles (or 100km) in a single ride is an achievable goal every cyclist can aspire to, and this scalable plan will help you reach it.

6 EXPERT LEVEL 6
Once you get beyond a century, you may want to push yourself even more. Events like Colorado's Leadville 100 mountain bike challenge, the Etape Du Tour—which allows regular riders to tackle a leg of the Tour de France—or even a double century (200 miles) are enormous challenges but also enormous fun. This program builds on the endurance built in Level 5 helping you create the fitness to tackle one of these iconic events.

ready to ride?

Eager to improve your fitness and have fun doing it? Fantastic! But before you swing your leg over the saddle and set off on your voyage of two-wheeled discovery, you really should ask yourself the following questions:

how's your health?

You may think you're pretty fit, or you may know you're really not. Whatever the case, though, since fitness and health are not the same, you should always visit your doctor and ask their opinion before starting any new exercise program.

how's your fitness?

Cycling can be as gentle or as demanding as you decide to make it, but you should be honest with yourself about your current capabilities in order to avoid disappointment at a very early stage. Use the "Key Requirements" for our different training plans (on pages 74–75) to guide you.

can I still ride?

Even if you consider yourself an experienced cyclist, if you haven't been on a bike for a while, your first ride should ideally be somewhere traffic-free and safe (a quiet, open grassy park would be ideal). Give yourself time to refresh basic skills like braking, changing gears, standing on the pedals, and cornering before you ride on open roads, all of which we'll cover in chapter four of this book.

what do I want to do?

We'll cover goal-setting and motivation in more detail over the next few pages, but it's worth considering that where you ride, what equipment you need, and even what sort of bike will suit you best will depend on what sort of riding you want to do. Use the introduction to the different sorts of cycling on pages 10–11 as a guide if you're undecided, and remember: you can always change your mind.

TEAM TACTICS

One excellent way to add enjoyment and expertise to your cycling is to join a local cycling group. Local bike shops will also know when and where rides take place in your area and whom to contact if you want to join in. You'll also find listings and advice online at www.usacycling.org. Some groups will focus on particular types of cycling, such as road, touring or mountain biking, so it's worth asking questions about their main interests to see if they match yours. Don't be afraid to try out several different groups to find the combination of riding style and people that suits you best.

BAR EXAMS

If you've never ridden a bike, it may be worth taking a cycling course with a qualified instructor. The League of American Bicyclists offers certified courses for children and adults; full details of which can be found online at www.bikeleague.org.

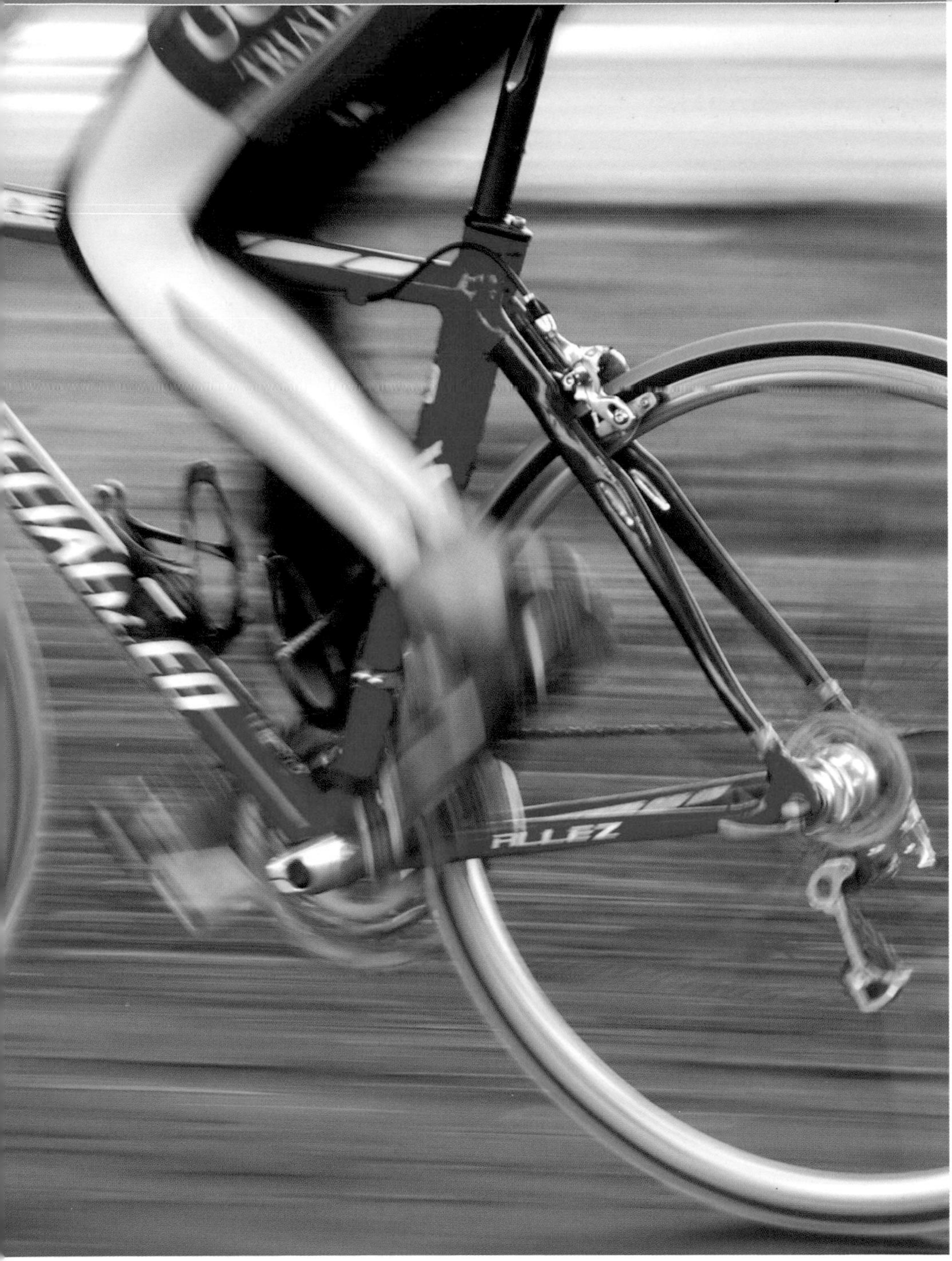
ALLEZ

going for goals

One of the best ways to make sure you get the most out of your cycling is to set yourself some clear and achievable – but also challenging – goals. The exact goals you choose are entirely up to you. It might be to ride for 30 minutes to the shops, or to train for a charity bike ride or even start racing. Once you have a target like this in mind you can also set yourself some less challenging milestones to mark your progress along the way. And remember, the best goals aren't just smart, they're SMARTER:

TIME IN THE SADDLE

Getting fitter, faster, and generally better at any activity takes time. It can take six to eight weeks to see measurable changes in your fitness, and they say it generally takes "seven times seven" repetitions to learn a new skill (and even longer to master it). Give yourself a break and don't expect perfection right from the start.

S=SPECIFIC

"To ride my bike" isn't a specific goal; "To build up until I am riding my bike for an hour three times a week" is. Make your goals clear and precise so you know where you're going.

M=MEASURABLE

Make sure your goals are measurable so you know when you've actually achieved them. Time and distance ridden, etc., are all very specific and easily tracked. Your means of measuring could be as simple as a wristwatch or on-the-bike speedometer to measure what you've done.

A=AGREED ON

It's much easier to stick to a plan when you have the support of those close to you, so talk to them about your plans and ask for their input and advice. Being accountable to someone for progress on your goals is a very helpful motivator, plus you never know, they might want to join in!

R=REALISTIC

Riding from Florida to California might sound like a fantastic idea (or not), but if you have not yet to the end of your street so far it might be a bit of a stretch! By all means, set goals that challenge your current limits, but don't go overboard. Use your goals as stepping stones, increasing the challenge as you go along.

T=TIME SPECIFIC

You'll find it much easier to motivate yourself if you set a date by which you must have achieved your goal. It's most effective to break your goals up into smaller milestones to be achieved each week, month and year so that they build on each other and keep you interested as time passes.

E=EXCITING

Choose goals that truly motivate you, and avoid ones that don't. They'll soon feel like drudgery and you won't stick with it. Sure, riding an exercise bike for thirty minutes a day will almost certainly make you fitter, but it'll also soon become boring. Find a goal that excites you and there's more chance you'll actually do it.

R=RECORDED

Make a note of your goals and put them somewhere you can see them every day (pinned to the fridge, on the monitor of your computer at work, or written on your calendar). That way you'll find it harder to 'forget' what you're hoping to achieve.

time management

We lead busy lives filled with work, family commitments, friends, chores and a hundred other distractions. This can make fitting in a regular exercise routine somewhat of a challenge. Indeed, there's no denying that if you want the fitness and sense of relaxation that regular cycling can give you, you may have to shuffle a few things around. Here are a few time-saving tips to make sure that any sacrifices you do make stay as small as possible.

rise earlier

If you're looking for more time in the day, consider adjusting your morning routine so that you can ride before you work. It's a great way to start the day energized and full of satisfaction, since your exercise is done before you even head to work.

prepare the night before

Hunting for your helmet and cleaning your bike when you're already supposed to be out the door are a waste of valuable time. Lay out exactly what you need to go riding in the morning at night before you go to bed, and get into the habit of wiping down your bike right after every ride. Keeping everything clean and organized is much easier if you stay on top of it.

agree to a routine

Exercising is much easier when you have the support of those around you. Either get them involved, too, or agree on a time when you're going to exercise that's convenient for everyone (perhaps while your partner's favorite TV show is on). Give a little consideration and all sorts of opportunities can open up.

exercise at lunchtime

If you're hoping to include some strength training in your weekly routine (see pages 64-71 to find out why you should), a short lunchtime session is a great way to fit it in. Hit the gym, train for 40 minutes, then head back to the office and eat lunch at your desk.

ditch the TV

The best way to free up large blocks of time in your schedule is to cut out TV watching. That is time that can be spent on the bike or doing other productive things. And after a year, what can you be more proud of? Watching a bunch of soon-forgotten shows, or being able to point to the many happy miles that you have put on your bike, along with your more healthy and fit body?

streamline other tasks

Cooking larger batches of food and then freezing individual portions, doing one big weekly shop rather than thousands of little trips...there are so many ways to combine cycling and other things, or to make everyday tasks more time-efficient. The only limit is your imagination.

COMMUTING BY BIKE

One of the most effective ways to slip cycling seamlessly into your everyday routine is to use your bicycle as a mode of transport. If you're going to try this it's usually best to start out by riding into work one day, and leaving the bike at the office overnight. Then ride your bike home the next day, taking the bus or train home or sharing a ride with a co-worker for the trips in-between. Build up gradually and you'll soon be able to ride both ways every day. Plus, it won't take long for you to figure out what you need at work and how to carry it to make commuting practical and fun.

TOP TIPS FOR COMMUTING

1 Equip your bike with decent LED lights (white for the front, red for the back), and carry spare batteries.

2 Opt for high-visibility clothing to wear while commuting. Yellow, orange, white, with reflective strips, all make you stand out.

3 Carry your change of clothes, lock, and other useful equipment in a backpack or courier bag.

4 Panniers are great on the bike but are rather cumbersome when you're not.

5 Invest in the best bike lock you can afford. A high-quality U lock is best. An even better option—see if your employer will allow you to bring your bike inside.

6 Make sure you carry a spare inner tube, tire levers, and a pump as part of your everyday commuting gear. Flats will happen.

7 Make sure that your bike is serviced regularly. You need your brakes to stop effectively, your tires to grip fully, and your gears to shift smoothly when riding in and around traffic.

8 If there are no showers at work, consider joining a nearby gym, shower there and then roll gently to the office. Otherwise, a few extra minutes for cool-down and then wiping down with a towel or baby-wipes works well.

9 **ALWAYS WEAR A HELMET!**

bikes and bits

From pedals to pumps and handlebars to helmets, this second chapter takes you on a tour of the world of cycling equipment. Inside you'll learn what to look for in a bicycle, how it ought to fit, and how to get the best bike for your money. You'll also find some suggestions on what sort of clothes to wear on the bike whatever the weather, and a few examples of what we'd consider must-have cycling accessories.

into the saddle

From the shiny high-tech carbon-fiber machines ridden by elite cyclists to the simple one-speed coaster, there are bikes out there for almost every imaginable speed, surface, purpose and mood. Broadly though they fall into one of four categories:

road bikes

Skinny tires, feather-light frames, and large wheels mean these bikes are easy to ride fast on paved streets. Don't be put off by the curly drop handlebars; they actually make it easier to handle the bike safely at higher speeds.

mountain bikes

Thick tires with plenty of tread, short and sturdy frames, and often some form of front or rear shocks to cushion your ride mean these bikes cope well with slippery, bumpy surfaces. Unfortunately, their weight, knobby tires, and small gears mean they're often hard to ride fast on the road.

city bikes

Sometimes called hybrids, city bikes combine the shape of a mountain bike with the gears and sometimes even wheel size of a road bike. They tend to offer a more upright riding position, which some people find more comfortable. One unusual subset of bikes in this category that may be of interest if you're hoping to commute is the folding bicycle, which are easier to take on the train or bus and carry to an upstairs apartment.

BMX bikes

Small, basic, agile, and very nearly indestructible, these bikes have only one gear and are designed for technical stunt riding rather than riding from place to place. The saddle heights on these bikes tend to be very low, as they're not intended for pedalling while sitting down.

BUYING A BIKE

Take a quick look around your local retailers or on the Internet and you'll soon realize that it's possible to buy bicycles all over the place, sometimes for very little money. But if you're hoping to use your bicycle as a way to get regular exercise, you should probably choose your bike with a little more care. First, you need to decide what sort of cycling you want to do. If you're going to ride entirely on the road, consider a road bike, or possibly a city bike. If you want to spend a lot of time off-road, riding dirt or gravel trails, consider buying a mountain bike. If you're not entirely sure but want the option to choose a variety of routes and rides, consider a mountain bike with front-suspension only and buy some slick road tires (or even a spare set of wheels) to swap as required.

BUYER'S GUIDE

1 Always buy your bicycle from a specialty bike shop instead of a big box retailer. The bikes carried by these mass-merchandisers are generally of lower quality, and sold by staff with limited knowledge of the bikes or how they should fit you. You'll find much better service and follow-up support from your local bike shop.

2 Do some research before you commit to a purchase. Look online and visit several different shops.

3 Set a budget before you start shopping, but always buy the best you can afford. $500–$1,000 should get you a good, long-lasting bike.

4 Ask about demo/floor bikes and last year's models. If you're not desperate for the current year's bike, you'll often find the previous one at a much better price.

5 Only buy from a shop that is able to fit you to a bicycle correctly. If they try to fit a bike to you simply by looking at your stand-over height (the clearance between you and the top tube of the bike) and nothing else, go somewhere else.

6 A bike fitting should involve looking at your saddle height, reach, and saddle position, and should take into account height, limb length, the type of bike, and even your health and how flexible you are.

are you sitting comfortably?

As we've already mentioned, a good bicycle shop should be able to fit you pretty precisely to a bike, but you may need to adjust it a bit more in certain places so that it's comfortable and efficient to ride. Here's how to fine-tune the key areas:

SEAT HEIGHT

Most new cyclists set their seat or saddle too low and then counteradjust it too high when they realize their mistake. To set your saddle height, remove your shoes and sit on your bike with one heel on a pedal (you'll need someone to hold the bike) and your hips level. Spin the pedals backwards until your pedal and crank are in line with the seat tube. If your leg is bent, raise the saddle until your leg is straight. If you can't reach the pedal with your heel without stretching, lower your saddle until you can. Remember to check both legs, as one may be slightly shorter than the other.

SADDLE POSITION

If your saddle is too far forward, you'll put pressure on your knees when pedalling; if it is too far back, you'll likely strain your lower back reaching for the handlebars. Get someone to hold your bike steady, then pedal backwards until your pedals are parallel to the floor. Sit square on your saddle with your hands on the handlebars and look down. The front of your leading knee should be in line with the axle in the middle of your pedal.

WHICH PART IS WHICH?

TOP TUBE

SEAT PIN

SEAT STAY

SEAT TUBE

HEAD TUBE

DOWN TUBE

CHAIN STAY

HANDLEBAR POSITION

Exactly what your ideal handlebar position will be depends on the sort of riding you're doing, your flexibility, and what you find comfortable. But as a general rule, the center of your handlebars should be at or below the level of your saddle, and you should be able to reach the handlebars comfortably with arms that are slightly bent.

The ride of your life

Two wheels, a frame, handlebars, a saddle, pedals. When you break it down, a bicycle is hardly a complicated machine. And there's no absolute need for you to know very much about all the different parts. That said, knowing how your brakes work, what your gears are, and the type of tires you'll need will all save you time and potentially money when the time comes to replace any worn-out parts.

1 SADDLE

Whether a particular type of saddle or seat is comfortable or not is a highly individual matter. What feels great to someone may be awful for you. If numbness or soreness prove to be an issue, look for a saddle with a cut-away center and be prepared to try several models. And whatever you chose, wear padded cycling shorts when riding for more than a few minutes, and get your saddle height correct (see pages 24-25) before you start riding.

2 TIRES

Different sorts of bike tires are available for riding on different sorts of terrain. Generally you want smoother tires for pavement and tires with more tread for dirt, sand or gravel surfaces. In any case, select a tire with a good level of puncture resistance, and remember that both the tires and inner tube sizes you need will be specific to the size of your wheels.

3 DERRAILEURS

These mechanisms, usually one in both front and back, move your chain across the cogs as you change gears. They play a big role in smooth shifting, and need to be kept clean and regularly oiled. They can get knocked out of alignment so try not to set your bike gear-side down.

4 BRAKES

Although some mountain bikes do have special disc brakes, most bicycle brakes use simple brake pads that press against the rim of the wheel to slow you down. The pads should be lined up so that they will press against the flat wall of the rim, and should be no more than two millimeters away from the metal.

5 HEADSET

Your headset is what allows you to steer your front wheel. The more you tighten it, the harder your handlebars will be to turn. If your headset is loose, it will feel like your handlebars are shifting backwards and forwards when you brake. If this happens, get an experienced mechanic to show you how to adjust it so that it's secure but not stiff.

6 CABLES

The cables that run from your brake levers and gear levers should be straight, unfrayed, and rust-free. They should remain taut as you change gears. If they lose tension and sag, it means they're sticking on something and may need replacing.

7 CHAIN

The chain on your bicycle is what transfers the power of your legs from the pedals to the rear wheel. Chains get dirty quickly, so wipe it clean and re-oil it after every ride where it has been exposed to significant dust, dirt or moisture, and clean it fully every two – three months. Over time your chain will also stretch and wear a surprising amount, so be prepared to replace it every year to 18-months (or every 2000-3000 miles) depending on the type of riding you do.

8 CASSETTE

Made up of small cogs called sprockets, your cassette is basically a stack of gears. The smaller the cog, the bigger and "harder" the gear. Like your chain, these need to be kept clean and oiled if they are to work properly.

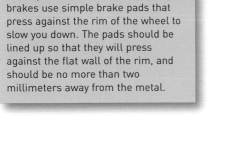

cycling essentials

Apart from a roadworthy bicycle, there are surprisingly few pieces of absolutely vital cycling equipment, but these are the things you really shouldn't be without.

HELMET

You don't have to wear a cycling helmet when riding, but it's certainly a good idea. The right fit is the most important feature. It should sit low across the brow, not tilted-up on the back of the head. The strap should be snug, with no more than a finger-width between the strap and your chin. The best helmets have adjustable cages that cradle the back of your skull. These can be tightened so that they hold the helmet securely on your head, yet still be adjusted as necessary for comfort or fit.

A CLEAN BIKE IS A HAPPY BIKE

One of the essentials we haven't mentioned here is that you must keep your bike clean. To find out why and how, turn to page 98.

BOTTLE AND CAGE

If you're riding for fitness you will need to drink while you cycle (see pages 42-43 for details of what, when and how much). A simple bottle cage that mounts on your down tube and a sports-style bottle offer the most convenient solution. Ideally buy a larger bottle (24 oz. is fairly common) rather than a small one. It's difficult to carry too much water, regardless of the length of the ride.

LIGHTS

You may have no intention at all of riding in the evening or night-time hours, but long stops, fixing flats, bad weather and other delays can leave you unexpectedly riding in the dark, so some small lights are good insurance. Look for small LED lights—a flashing red one that you can secure below your seat at the back, and a bright white one on your handlebars at the front. Technology is evolving so that extremely bright, rechargeable LED lights are now quite affordable. These are ideal if you plan to ride in the evening or in areas without street lights.

PUNCTURE REPAIR KIT

Flat tires are an inevitable part of cycling. Sooner or later you'll have to fix one during a ride (and you'll find tips on doing so on pages 96-97). You can find pocket-sized patch kits with patches, glue, sandpaper and such, and try to repair the tire on the road. However, many cyclists simply prefer to carry a spare inner tube, some strong plastic tire levers in a jersey pocket or in a bag under your saddle and simply swap out the tube, opting to repair the puncture itself back home.

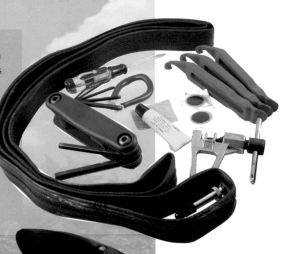

PUMP

If you're riding regularly, you may find that you'll ultimately want to have two different pumps. One will be the larger floor-standing pump that you use to air up your tires at home; the other is a smaller, high-pressure pump that mounts on your bike frame, carried with you to use on the road in case of flats while riding.

summer clothing

Summer cycling apparel needs to be light, flexible, and breathable. It's almost always made of technical fabrics that pull sweat away from the skin, keeping you as dry and chafe-free as possible.

From replica team uniforms to colorful jerseys carrying logos of beer brands and rock bands to specially tailored cycling bottoms, tops and jackets, you can find cycling wear these days to suit just about every taste and budget. Realistically, you could wear just about anything to go riding, but proper cycling clothes are comfortable, practical and long-lasting. Here are a few examples of what to look for:

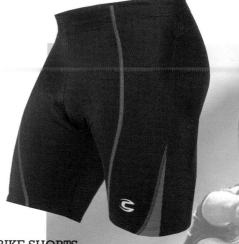

DRESSING FOR SUMMER

1 **Get technical**
Choose synthetic material over cotton, which holds moisture and leads to chafing. Shirts and tops come from an array of manufacturers, so don't limit yourself to cycling specific brands. Though these materials can cost more, they more than make up for the price difference with the durability, versatility and comfort they offer.

2 **Dare to bare**
Once you're warmed up and rolling along, long-pant leg and long-sleeve tops will make you real warm, real fast. Go for short sleeves and shorts, and carry a light top-layer folded up in a pocket that you can wear as needed.

3 **Protect yourself**
The breeze may make you feel cooler as you ride, but remember that bare skin and hot sun don't mix well. Apply sunscreen before you ride, and carry a small tube in your jersey pocket on longer rides. You can reapply as necessary during breaks.

BIKE SHORTS

Cycling shorts come in any number of lengths, colors and fits—they don't even have to be tight Lycra. What you will need, however, is a pair of shorts that have a comfortable pad sewn into the crotch and seat. Look for pads that are gender-specific, and buy as good a pair of shorts as you can afford. Your cycling shorts may be the single most important factor to enjoying comfortable riding.

SPORTS BRA

Bending forward over the handlebars will put a lot of strain on the Cooper's Ligament, particularly if the road surface is bumpy, and this can lead to entirely avoidable soreness. For this reason alone, proper sports bras are a must for the ladies.

CYCLING SOCKS

Experienced cyclists frequently find that they prefer short, snug-fitting socks like distance runners wear. Short socks help keep you cool and ones with a snug fit will help avoid blisters. The technical material used also helps shed moisture, another factor in blister prevention.

CYCLING JERSEY

A cycling top made from a technical fabric is a much more comfortable alternative to a simple T-shirt. Cycling jerseys often have useful pockets along the back, which are great for keeping keys, cell phones, and other essential items out of the way of your legs when you pedal. Look for one with short sleeves and at least a half-length zipper so that you have the option to open it if it's really hot.

CYCLING GLOVES

Lightweight, fingerless cycling gloves will protect your hands from the shock of any rough roads and will stop you from slipping on the handlebars if you get wet or sweaty. Look for gloves with gel padding in the heel of the palm and the area around the thumb and forefinger.

winter clothing

For most of us, winter wardrobe means bundling up. But when you're on your bike in the winter, your heaviest sweater and thickest winter coat is not really what you want.

Your winter cycling wear should focus on layers and still contain lots of technical materials, since you are still pedaling and will still sweat from the exertion. A bit of wool mixed in will help keep you warm, and it has its own natural wicking properties. You'll also need some items of clothing that are windproof and waterproof too.

DRESSING FOR WINTER

1 **beat the windchill**
Cycling generates quite a breeze even on the calmest days, and in winter this can really increase the wind chill. But you can certainly help keep yourself warm with the layering techniques described here plus a nice outer windproof jacket. Clothing made from Gore-Tex and other warm yet breathable materials offer the most efficient protection.

2 **cover up**
Make sure your hands, feet, head, and especially your ears are covered before you go off riding in cold weather, because your exposed extremities are most vulnerable when the temperature drops.

3 **pack a poncho**
Carry a lightweight waterproof rain jacket/poncho if you think there's even the slightest chance of rain or snow during your ride. These too stow compactly in a pocket and are invaluable in case the weather turns bad. Being on the bike when you're cold and soaked-through is neither healthy nor much fun.

HAT OR HEADBAND

Often wearing a hat is the biggest factor in helping keep yourself warm. Your ears are particularly vulnerable to suffering from winter winds. Because of this, you'll find a simple, stretchy wool or Lycra skullcap or ear-warmer to be a must-have in winter. Even in the cold you'll find yourself soaking these with sweat as you ride, so it is worth having a couple if you're riding daily so they can dry out between uses.

BASE LAYER

A tight-fitting, technical undershirt will wick sweat away from your skin before it cools and makes you cold. Wool is a good choice too, for it has excellent wicking and insulating properties. For maximum versatility, look for a short-sleeved one that you can wear alone under your jersey on autumn days or paired with arm warmers (see below) as a makeshift long-sleeved base on colder days.

LONG-SLEEVE JACKET

Winter versions of cycling jerseys range from simple, long-sleeved versions of summer shirts to heavy-duty, fleece-lined, wind-proof winter jackets. If you can afford it, it's worth having both so you can cope in a range of conditions.

ARM AND LEG WARMERS

A smart and versatile addition to your cool-weather riding gear are arm and leg warmers. These simple Lycra tubes can be pulled on or off your bare arms and legs like socks as the temperature changes while you're riding. These stow conveniently in your pocket and are the type of thing you'll never regret having along. Be sure to actually try on your first pair before you buy rather than guessing at the size. Having some that droop and sag while you ride because they're too big can be maddening!

WINTER GLOVES

Good gloves are another necessity in the winter, simply because your hands are exposed on the handlebars. Skiing or snowboarding gloves work well, but make sure you can still operate your brakes and shifters while wearing them.

LIGHT VEST

A simple, lightweight, sleeveless jacket is a good piece of an emergency kit to stash in a pocket. Look for one with a windproof front and a shower-proof coating that'll double as a waterproof.

WOOL SOCKS

There's no way to guarantee dry feet in wet weather, but with technical or Merino wool socks your feet should at least stay a little warmer. Try layering two pairs to help keep your feet even warmer.

useful tools

From bells to baskets to bottle holders, there's a whole industry supplying accessories and gadgets designed to enhance your riding experiences. Leaving aside some of the more wacky options, here are a few examples of items that may really come in handy:

SHOES AND CLIPLESS PEDALS

Wearing bike shoes that attach you to your pedals may sound unnerving, but they can make a noticeable boost to your speed and efficiency. There are many different styles of shoe and pedal combinations, so you're sure to find something to suit your needs. Just be aware that it can be tricky to get in and out at first, so practicing in a nice soft grassy area is a good way to get accustomed to them.

REPAIR AND REPLACE

Even if it sees only light use, some parts of your bicycle will eventually wear out. Replace your chain every year or two and your gear and brake cables at the same interval (or sooner if these parts get rusty). You'll know your brake pads need replacement when they reach the wear mark on the side. If in doubt, take your bike into your local cycle shop at the beginning of every riding season and ask them to service it for you more often if you ride in frequently wet or dirty conditions.

FENDERS

Cheap, light front and rear fenders are a happy thing for you, your bike, your clothes, and anyone riding behind you when it's wet. You can get fenders that are permanently mounted, or a set with quick release mounts for easy on/off.

SUNGLASSES

Sunglasses help cyclists in several ways. They shade from glare on bright days, but also help keep your eyes from drying out from the wind. Glasses with photochromatic lenses are particularly helpful. They darken in sunlight but stay clear on cloudy days and evenings. When shopping for sunglasses, try on several pairs while wearing your cycling helmet to make sure you buy a pair that are both comfortable and compatible with the fit of your helmet.

CYCLE COMPUTER

Having a basic bike speedometer (or "cyclocomputer") is perhaps one of the first accessories you'll want to purchase. Relatively inexpensive, these will give you immediate detail on your present speed, total distance ridden, your average speed, maximum speed, and how long your ride has taken. Higher-end models can track your pedaling cadence, and you can even get ones with GPS systems and maps to guide you on new routes or that interface with your heart-rate monitors (see below).

HEART RATE MONITOR

If you're serious about using your bike to develop your fitness, a heart rate monitor is a great idea. A strap worn around your chest records your heart rate and sends the data to a wristwatch or cycle computer. If you know your maximum heart rate and heart rate training zones (see pages 72-73), you can use the information displayed to keep your effort even despite the changing terrain and weather conditions.

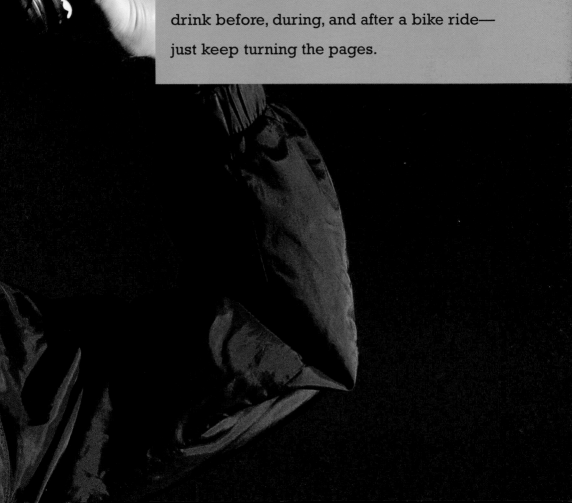

food for thought

If you want to ride well, you need to eat well. To find out what's good (and what's not) for fueling your body and how much of it you're going to need—as well as tips on what and how much to drink, dietary supplements you might want to consider, and how to eat and drink before, during, and after a bike ride— just keep turning the pages.

food for thought

Eating and cycling, or indeed form of activity, have a complex relationship. On the one hand, we're often working out to lose a bit of extra weight, but on the other hand you can't cycle for very long if your body has no stored energy. Over the next few pages you'll find information about the different food groups and how your body uses them and how much food you'll need per day, as well as a few tips on how to eat healthy. We'll also talk about what, when, and how much to eat in and around your bike rides.

FOOD GROUPS

All food contains a combination of five different types of fuel—carbohydrates, protein, fat, water, and trace nutrients. Here's a look at what each one does and what your best sources are:

CARBOHYDRATES

Broadly speaking, there are two types of carbohydrate: sugars, which provide easy-to-burn, short bursts of energy, and starches, which burn more gradually and provide a sustained release of fuel for your body.
Aim to get 60 percent of your daily calories from carbohydrates.

PROTEIN

If carbohydrates are what our bodies use for fuel, protein is what the engine is made of. After every ride our muscles and tendons are rebuilt slightly stronger and are slightly more efficient at using the protein we eat. And since our bodies can't store protein, it's very important that your post-ride meal or snack includes a source of high-quality protein like meat, fish, or even egg whites.
Aim to get 20 percent of your daily calories from protein.

FAT

We're bombarded with things telling us how bad fat is and how important it is to eat a low fat diet. While it's certainly true that some fats are extremely bad for you and should be avoided as much as possible (hydrogenated fats and trans fatty acids in particular), mono- and polyunsaturated fats are in fact beneficial to our overall health. (For practical advice on what fats to eat, turn the page).
Aim to get 20 percent of your daily calories from healthy fats

WATER

Water is absolutely essential for life. Lose just one percent of your body's water and your mental and physical performance may drop by up to 10 percent. Surprisingly, there's water in almost every food we eat, but you'll still need to drink regularly to ensure that you have enough.

TRACE ELEMENTS

Vitamins, minerals, phytochemicals, and antioxidants—there's much more in fresh unprocessed food. These chemicals are only needed in tiny amounts, but they perform a range of functions from boosting our immune system to helping us burn fuel more effectively. Thankfully, a varied diet that's rich in fresh fruits and vegetables should provide most of these without any trouble, but it's worth taking a daily multivitamin just to be sure, particularly if you're planning a lot of cycling.

healthy eating

Now that you know how your body uses food, it's time to consider how much you need and what types of foods you should choose when shopping, cooking, or dining out. So, if you need to improve your diet and perhaps shed a few excess pounds, here's a look at what you should be eating:

A PRACTICAL FOOD PYRAMID

The lower down on the pyramid a type of food is, the more of it you should be aiming to eat.

TOP LAYER

Candy, cakes, pastry, cookies and chips—try to avoid having these regularly. Ideally, aim for no more frequently than once every other day, and ideally only in small servings. That may sound rough, but if you're looking to sharpen your nutrition, that's the first place to find progress.

SECOND LAYER

Healthy fats. Go for small amounts of calorie-dense foods like salmon, mackerel, avocados, olive oil, nuts and seeds, and steer clear of butter, margarine, or corn oil. Two or three eggs a week won't hurt, either.

THIRD LAYER

Quality proteins like skinless chicken, white fish, grass-fed beef and lean cuts of other meats. Grill, stew, steam or stir-fry these foods rather than frying them in lots of oil.

FOURTH LAYER

Whole grain breads and pastas, brown and basmati rice, beans and sweet potatoes—try to pick these rather than highly processed white bread, pasta, and rice, and avoid dishes that are fried or served with oil or cream sauces.

BOTTOM LAYER

Fruit and vegetables—fresh or frozen are best, but even canned in water or juice (not syrup or oil), these foods are your friends. If you need a snack, reach for these. Try to get four varied servings of fruit and vegetables every day.

YOUR DAILY BREAD

How much you need to eat each day depends on three factors. Use these simple formulas to work out how many calories you actually need.

1
As a general rule, women tend to need fewer calories than men.
Men: Your basic requirement is 11calories per pound of bodyweight (24 kcal/kg).
Women: Your basic requirement is 10 calories per pound (or 22 kcal/kg).
This is just to fuel your body in its basic state.

2
Of course, how active you are in your everyday life also has an impact too.

Add an extra 30–40 percent of your first number if you spend most of the day sitting, even at work.

Add an extra 50–60 percent if you're always on the go (e.g., if you work in construction).

The more exercise you do. the more calories you need.
Add 400 kcal per hour of cycling you do.

3
So, that means a 160 lb. male accountant will need 2376 calories (160 lbs x 11 = 1760 to support basic living, then 616 more (0.35 x 1760)) – on a day when he doesn't cycle, and 2776 on a day where he rides for an hour.

And that's just to stay even. Weight loss begins when calories consumed in food are less than what gets burned each day.

water relief

Back on page 39, we explained how important water is for staying healthy and even staying alive. Despite knowing this, many people still don't achieve the level of daily fluid intake they need. Here are seven simple tricks that you can use to make sure you get enough to drink:

DRINKING MORE WATER

1 Drink a small (8 oz.) glass of water every morning when you get up.

2 Drink something every time you eat.

3 Carry a bottle of water with you whenever you leave the house.

4 Aim to drink between around 16-24 oz. of water each hour when cycling (the hotter it is, the more you will need).

5 Drink a glass of water before you go to bed each night.

6 When the weather is hot, keep a bottle of water beside your bed and drink if you wake in the middle of the night feeling thirsty.

7 Remember that fresh fruits and vegetables contain lots of water, so make sure you get all your portions each day.

HYDRATION Q & A

Even after you've looked at your approach to drinking, there's more you can do. Here's a run-through of some common daily drinks and the issues and problems that surround them.

BEERS, WINES, AND SPIRITS

Good news! Research has shown that small amounts of certain alcoholic drinks can have positive effects on our health. That means that the occasional beer or glass of wine with dinner is fine, but do be aware that large amounts of alcohol can have negative effects on your ability to exercise safely and effectively in both the short and long term.

COFFEE BREAKS

Coffee and tea are often frowned upon because the caffeine they contain is a diuretic, which means it can encourage your body to pass too much water. But, in truth, the amounts of caffeine in these drinks are far outweighed by the amount of liquid in them, so they're unlikely to leave you dehydrated if you're drinking enough. Plus, studies have shown generally that caffeine has a positive effect on both athletic and mental activity.

COLAS AND OTHER CARBONATED DRINKS

If you're drinking lots of soda, this is where you might consider making a change in your diet. They hold lots of empty calories, and even if you opt for the diet version, the artificial sweeteners used in them are not the nicest things to put into your system. Plus they tend to be quite acidic, which isn't good for your teeth. So, if you want to treat yourself to the occasional soda, by all means, knock yourself out. Just remember it's a treat and that it's best to avoid making them a big part of your liquid intake, even if they are diet.

A NEW SQUEEZE

Fruit juice is a disappointingly ambiguous drink. It's undoubtedly better for you than soda, but if you're trying to lose weight it can be a surprising source of hidden calories and sugars, especially if you're chugging a bunch on a hot day. As a rule, whole fresh fruit are better than juices, and freshly squeezed juices are better than those preserved in bottles or cans. Check the bottle or carton ingredients carefully, too. Proper fruit juice should be just that—100% juice without lots of added sugar or sweetener.

supplements

There are your standard vitamins and minerals, then there are all the other things you can add to your diet to supposedly make all sorts of things better. Bee pollen, St. John's Wort, acai berries, ginseng, and wheat germ . . . the sheer array of non-medical dietary supplements sold online and in stores is astounding. Unfortunately the evidence supporting many of their claims is quite varied, and this can make it hard to decide what—if anything— you should consider taking. With that in mind, here's a look at a several supplements in particular that you might consider taking to enhance your health and perhaps also improve your cycling.

FOR MAINTENANCE:
Multivitamin and mineral complex
Ensuring that your daily diet contains all the things you need, in the right amounts, every day can be difficult. For this reason alone taking a good-quality one-a-day multivitamin is a good idea. You can find versions specifically formulated for your age and gender that give you the basic nutrients you need without going overboard.

FOR OVERALL HEALTH:
Omega 3 fish oils
Regular doses of two particular omega 3s—EPA and DHA—seem to have an array of health benefits that are worth having. They help keep your heart healthy, regulate blood triglyceride levels, improve circulation and nerve function, combat the symptoms of arthritis, and even protect the brain from diseases like Alzheimer's and Parkinson's. On top of all this, their anti-inflammatory effects may even help you recover more quickly after exercise. Aim for 1000–2000 mg per day.

FOR FEWER JOINT ACHES:
Glucosamine sulphate
Quite commonly taken as a treatment for osteoarthritis, glucosamine is one supplement that teeters on the edge of medical acceptance. In Europe, glucosamine is approved as a medical drug and is sold in the form of glucosamine sulphate, while in the United States, the FDA has not approved it as a medical supplement. Since glucosamine is derived from shellfish, you may wish to avoid it if you're allergic to shellfish—though it is derived from the shells of these animals, not the flesh where the allergen exists.

FOR BURNING MORE FAT:
Green tea supplements
Among the most unusual but possibly useful supplements on the market are green tea tablets. Most studies have investigated its apparent anti-cancer and antioxidant properties, but there's also evidence to suggest that high doses (around 1000 mg) of green tea (equivalent to drinking about a quart of actual green tea) may improve your body's ability to burn fat as fuel by up to 20 percent. Again, this hasn't been officially confirmed by sufficient research at this time to endorse this claim, but a number of studies have suggested its several positive effects.

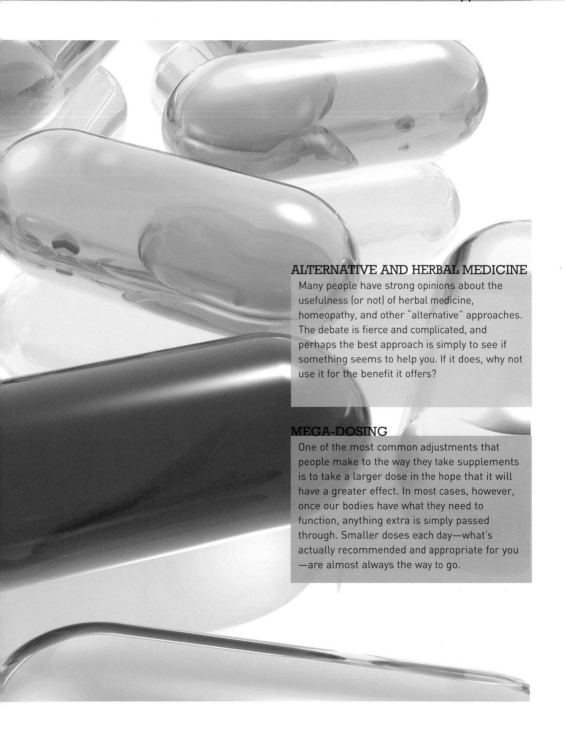

ALTERNATIVE AND HERBAL MEDICINE

Many people have strong opinions about the usefulness (or not) of herbal medicine, homeopathy, and other "alternative" approaches. The debate is fierce and complicated, and perhaps the best approach is simply to see if something seems to help you. If it does, why not use it for the benefit it offers?

MEGA-DOSING

One of the most common adjustments that people make to the way they take supplements is to take a larger dose in the hope that it will have a greater effect. In most cases, however, once our bodies have what they need to function, anything extra is simply passed through. Smaller doses each day—what's actually recommended and appropriate for you —are almost always the way to go.

meals on wheels

A balanced, healthy diet is important for everyone, but if you're riding your bike the amounts and timing of what you eat and drink may need to change. Here's a timeline for how to best fuel your body before, during, and after a ride.

2 hours before

This is the latest time you can eat a proper meal. Digesting lots of solid food diverts blood flow away from the muscles, so you need to leave enough time between your meal and your ride for the food to go down.

30 minutes before

If you haven't eaten for two or three hours before you ride, you may want to consider eating a small snack now. A simple snack of fruit, a low-fat yogurt, or some cereal with skim milk is ideal.

during your ride

Okay, let's acknowledge right now that you may not ride like Lance Armstrong, but that doesn't mean you can't learn lessons from the way pro cyclists like him fuel themselves. Any ride lasting over an hour is a ride that is best done with fuel. What sort of fuel? You can eat bananas, pretzels, chewy candies, and even good-old PBJ sandwiches, but for more effective fuels, look at the "Alternative Fuels" panel to the right.

within 20 minutes of finishing

After a long or hard ride your body will be crying out to refuel. But this doesn't mean you should reach for the first fried or chocolate thing you find on the rack at the convenience store. What your body needs is a combination of carbohydrates and a serving of protein to help speed both the refueling and rebuilding processes. You can get these easily from proper sports recovery drinks or, at a pinch, from small meals like scrambled eggs on toast or granola stirred in with low-fat yogurt.

later that day

Long rides in particular can take you right to the edge of your fuel supplies no matter how carefully you refuel. This can lead to some unexpected sugar cravings even hours after your ride. If at all possible, try to avoid the temptation to hit the fried stuff and sweets and turn instead to balanced, healthy meals which contain lean proteins, whole grain carbohydrates and plenty of fresh vegetables and fruit.

DRINK UP!

Remember, no matter how long you ride, you should be drinking while you do it. Take a full bottle of water with you on even the shortest rides. And hit it frequently!

ALTERNATIVE FUELS

There are lots of sports drinks and energy foods on the market that have been specially designed with cyclists, runners and triathletes in mind. While they may not be as natural as an apple or as inviting as a blueberry muffin, they are carefully developed to give you what you need during exercise. Sports drinks contain electrolytes to replenish the salts you lose while sweating. If the taste or sweetness of the full-strength version of these are too strong, you can certainly dilute them with water as needed. Also, energy gels and bars are easy to use and convenient to stick in your jersey pocket. But they are expensive and probably not necessary unless you're headed out for a multi-hour, medium-to high-intensity ride.

ride fit skills

Braking, cornering, climbing hills, and changing gears… The simple primers in this chapter will introduce the commonly overlooked skills that form the basis of safe cycling. Over the next few pages you'll also find out how to use weight training, stretching, and core stability development to enhance both your general and bike-specific fitness.

ride skills—braking

It will come as no great shock to hear that the ability to stop your bike without crashing into something is a key skill in cycling. What you may find surprising, however, is how many bike riders aren't particularly good at stopping their bike safely and under control. This simple skill could—quite literally—save your life. Here's how to do it:

braking to stop

While remaining seated, gently squeeze both brake levers at the same time. Don't use just one brake —if you smash down on the front brake by itself, it'll buck you over the handlebars; jamming the back brake only will lock up your rear wheel into a skid. Always apply both together. Until you're used to your bike it's also a good idea to brake a little earlier than you need to. Better to stop too soon that too late!

braking to slow down

If you want to slow yourself down some, but not stop, you can use a technique called "feathering" the brakes to scrub off some speed. To do this, stop pedaling and apply both brakes very gently so that they just brush the rims of your wheels, then release. You can repeat this as necessary until you reach the desired speed.

breaking at speed

Let's say you're riding fast and need to stop suddenly. An effective technique is to shift your weight back on your saddle as far as you

comfortably can. This will improve the traction of your back wheel and help you stay balanced. Everything else about stopping at speed stays the same. You simply do it faster.

LOOKING AFTER YOUR BRAKES

You'll find that you use your brakes a lot when you ride, and so the brake pads will eventually wear out and need replacing. But even before that point, regular maintenance and inspection are important too, so that your brakes keep functioning well during routine use.

BEFORE EACH RIDE

Check that your brakes are in line with the rims and set no farther than ⅛ inch out.

AFTER EACH RIDE

Check your rims for scratches along the path of the brakes. Long scratches usually mean there's a rock, piece of glass or wire stuck in the brake pad that you'll have to dig out to avoid damage to your rims.

BE ALERT!

Regardless of what manuever you are going to make on the road—slowing, turning, changing lanes, etc.,—always be aware of what is behind and in front of you, and signal your action to others (pages 58-59). Never assume that people are completely aware of your presence. Take responsibility for your safety whenever you ride, wherever you ride.

WHICH ONE'S WHICH?

In standard installation practice in the U.S., the left-hand brake lever controls your front brake, and your right-hand lever your back brake. If in doubt, simply stand astride your bike and try squeezing each brake lever in turn. You should be able to see the brakes engage as you work the levers. If you are still in doubt, fully squeeze the left brake lever and try to push the bike forward. When the front brake is engaged performing this action will raise your back wheel off the floor. If you're squeezing the rear brake, the rear wheel will not turn but rather slide as you push the bike forward.

ride skills—cornering

The sight of a whole pack of pro cyclists whipping around a curve at speeds in excess of 35 mph as they stream toward the finish is one of the most amazing scenes in cycling. The speeds are so high, and the bikes are so close that it seems incredible that they don't all crash into each other. You may not start out as fast as them, and you may never find yourself cornering in the middle of a tightly packed mass of riders, but smooth, efficient cornering is a vital skill that every rider should learn.

steering around corners
The most straightforward way to corner is simply to turn your handlebars in the direction of the corner and pedal around the corner. While this might seem the best, safest way to corner, it can actually leave you surprisingly unbalanced, since your wheels are no longer running in the same direction.

leaning through corners
The most effective way to corner involves little thinking, but just to simply treat your body and your bike as a single unit and let gravity and momentum do the rest. Here's a step-by step look at what actually happens when you approach turns this way:

U-TURNS

Being able to steer sharp corners smoothly without putting your feet down will give you a finer appreciation of the subtleties of balancing your bike, and a useful ability to steer around obstacles when you need to. Practice this skill on a very quiet road, or even on some dry, short-cut, level grass, and wear normal shoes rather than cycling shoes at first, as you'll find it easier to put a foot down if you need to. Like any other cornering, turn at a speed you're confident with, look where you're going as you gently steer the bars, lean the bike slightly, and press your outside foot down into the pedal.

LEANING

As you enter the turn, scan the road surface ahead for any holes, grit or obstacles you want to avoid.

Pick your path through the turn based on both what you see and any traffic around you.

If you feel you need to brake, do so gently before you start to lean into the corner.

Look along the road, through the corner in the direction you want to go

Press your outside foot down so the pedal sits at the bottom of the stroke and lean the bike and your body together in the direction of the turn.

Coast through the turn with no more braking unless necessary until you are all the way through the corner.

For faster turns, try to take it through the corner using as straight an arc as possible. One trick is to swing out into the road as far as is safe before you enter the corner, and then swoop back in sharply to follow a line that cuts directly across the turn. Doing this will take you very near the curb/inside part of the corner as you swing through the center.

Note: this is a racing technique and may not be the smartest way to handle riding your bike in city traffic.

ride skills—changing gear

Bicycles have had gears for a very long time now, but a surprising number of seasoned riders still don't know how to use them properly. The strange thing is, it's actually very simple. Rather than worrying about what the "right" gear is that you should ride in, try to picture instead what it feels like when you're riding using the pedal speed and effort in which you feel most comfortable. This is called your "cadence," the speed (measured in revolutions per minute) at which your pedals go round. Typical cadence varies from cyclist to cyclist, but 80-100 rpm is common.

The basic principle to understand about gears is that they are what give you the ability to pedal that same comfortable pace and effort, regardless of if you're climbing a steep incline, riding on flat ground, or going down a big hill. Your speed will vary quite a bit of course but your cadence and effort should be about the same regardless, all thanks to your gears, which you adjust by shifting into higher or lower gears as needed.

Of course, this supposes you know the ins and outs (or really ups and downs) of how your gears work, so here's a basic guide.

big and little

Your bike will likely have gear shifters on both sides of your handlebar. One set (usually the right hand one) will work the small gears on your back wheel. The other (usually the left) will work the larger gears up near your pedals. To figure out which is which, simply pick the back wheel off the ground and flip one of the gear shifters while spinning the pedals forward. You should hear and/or see the chain move from one gear to another either in front by the pedals or on the sprockets on your back wheel, and this will give you the answer.

The gears on your rear wheel are what you should use to shift most frequently. There are smaller adjustments between these gears, and frequent shifting here will accommodate most changes in terrain. The chain rings up front are for major shifts, such as between riding on the flats and then climbing a big hill. Shifting between chain rings in front adjusts the range that your rear gears can handle.

using your gears

You should be using your gears a lot every ride. Unless you're on completely flat ground, you'll find yourself shifting frequently, especially on the rear sockets where the adjustments are smaller from one to another. This is the right approach, even when you want to speed up. Many cyclists who want to go faster simply dump themselves into the biggest, hardest gear they have and try to thump along by mashing down hard on the pedals. You're better off slightly increasing your cadence first, and only then moving to a bigger gear as required.

mastering your gears

The best way to develop your ability to use your gears subtly is to ride an undulating to hilly route and to shift gears as necessary to maintain that constant, smooth effort and cadence. After a few tries you'll realize that on down hills you have to move from a small to a large gear at the front, but that as you do so you also need to adjust the small gears at the back (usually making it easier) to keep everything smooth, and that the reverse is true when climbing.

ANTICIPATION IS KEY

One of the keys to shifting effectively is to anticipate the need to change gears and plan accordingly. Since it's very hard on your bike (and you!) to shift when you're applying a lot of pressure to the pedals, shifting just before it really gets tough helps avoid all that strain. So be thinking of a downshift as you approach a stop sign or big hill, and you can solve many problems by avoiding them altogether.

BIG, LITTLE, EASY, HARD

The words used to describe a gear can be a bit tricky. "Downshifting" means to put your bike in a lower gear, which makes it easier to pedal, but you won't go as fast. Conversely, shifting into a higher gear will make it feel harder to pedal, but gives more speed.

ride skills—handling skills

Going up and coming down hills are two of the most fulfilling and (if you choose) demanding aspects of cycling. Here's how to do them:

CLIMBING

Speak to many cyclists and they speak in hushed tones about hills and high mountains. There seems to be a belief that hills are necessarily hard work. This is both right and wrong. On the one hand, you will have to work harder to maintain a given speed up a climb because you're working against gravity; on the other hand, almost all bikes have an array of gears. And this is the secret of climbing—because you have gears it doesn't have to be hard. Most of the problems that people have with hills come from trying to chase other riders or riding too hard at the start of a climb.

How to climb

Ride to the bottom of the climb at your normal effort and cadence, and as the road starts to rise, gradually down shift down through the gears so that you keep your cadence and effort as even as possible. Stay seated as you climb and only stand on the pedals if you have to (standing uses a lot more energy than sitting). Forget about your speed and concentrate on maintaining a smooth cadence and an even effort. You're not racing, so pace yourself and use your gears to maintain your cadence as the gradient changes. Lots of bikes offer a "granny gear" on the rear wheel, which is a sprocket designed just for climbing, so it makes the pedaling easy enough that you'll be able to keep going up just about any incline, no matter how steep. You won't be going fast at all, but hey, you're still going.

CLIMBING GEAR

If you're planning a particularly hilly or mountainous route, make extra sure that your brakes and gears are clean and working properly. Always wear a helmet, and think about putting on an extra layer and gloves before you begin a long descent, as the wind can be quite chilly at high speeds. Sunglasses are a smart idea too, as the wind on a fast downhill run can dry out your eyes quickly.

HOW TO DESCRIBE A HILL OR ROUTE

Flat—no more than a few short, gentle changes in gradient.

False flat—a visually unnoticeable but physically very obvious slight slope.

Undulating—a series of short, not too steep hills and descents with very little flat in between.

Rolling—much like "undulating" but the climbs will probably be steeper.

Hilly—exactly that; the route contains some large (for the area) hills, though there may be flat, undulating, or rolling parts in between.

Mountainous—long climbs up mountains and similarly long, winding descents; often not nearly as steep as shorter climbs.

DESCENDING

Freewheeling down a hill in the bright sunshine is a glorious experience, but if you're unprepared it can also be a scary one. Ultimately, though, the skills for descending are the skills of braking and cornering done at higher speeds, so if you're confident with them you should soon be confident on the down-hills, too.

How to descend

Sit solidly at the center or back of your saddle and relax. Place your hands at a loose, ready position on your brake levers. Focus your eyes on the road ahead of you, looking for corners, changes in gradient, potholes, water, and gravel. If you need to slow yourself, remember to keep your weight back and to brake gently and smoothly, ideally before you hit any corners. Above all, never force your pace beyond where you are comfortable.

ride skills—riding with others

Sooner or later you'll find yourself riding with other people. You might head out with friends, join an organized ride, or strike up a conversation with people you meet out on the road. When this happens, here are a few things to keep in mind to make the group riding experience safer and more enjoyable for everyone.

Groups of cyclists usually ride in pairs, though laws vary from place to place about what's permitted on public streets as far as riding abreast. Wherever you are in the group, stay shoulder to shoulder with the rider beside you and as close to them as you both feel comfortable. If there's a rider in front of you, follow directly behind their back wheel, again as close as is comfortable, even around corners. Frequently this can be as little as 6-12 inches back. If you're at the front of the group, ride at an even pace and as straight a line as you can—twitching and weaving can be difficult for the group to follow. It's irritating for the other riders and the accordion effect that results is a frequent cause of crashes.

riders of differing abilities

One of the most challenging things is when riders of differing abilities get together. It can be a frustrating experience for all involved. But, with a little bit of thought and consideration, even this situation can still be enjoyable.

If you're one of the strongest riders in a group, keep your effort nice and even, especially up and over hills. If people have trouble keeping up, ride in a smaller gear with a higher cadence. This will slow you down and make you work harder at the same time. If people drop right off the back, slow down, coast, and wait for them—it's what you'd want someone to do for you.

If everyone in the group seems much faster than you, don't worry, but do let them know. Try not to ride on the front of the group, but don't sit on the back either because you'll find that the slight changes in tempo through turns and over hills will soon wear you out as you push to catch up. The best place to be is in the middle of the group, tucked in nice and tight

behind a slightly stronger rider who can help pull you along. If you start to fall back tell someone and ask them to ease back the pace a bit—better that than that having them look back at some point to find that you've long since disappeared!

safety

Everyone in a group is responsible not just for their own safety but also for the safety of their fellow riders. If you see or hear a car approaching, call out "car back" or "car up" as appropriate. Similarly, if you spot a pot hole, gravel, or some other obstacle, point it out so that everyone in the group can avoid it. The box below shows you some common hand signals to use in a group ride. Teach them to riders who don't know them, both by explaining and through your own example of using them—it'll help keep everyone safe.

CYCLING HAND SIGNALS

1 **right arm pointing out sideways** = turn right
left arm pointing out sideways = turn left

2 **pointing your right hand down to the road surface beside your leg** = obstacle on the road on your right side

3 **pointing your left hand down to the road surface beside your leg** = obstacle on the road on your left side

4 Holding a spread palm down by your leg but facing backwards = slow down

5 Tucking an arm behind your back = Stationary or slow-moving object on that side (e.g., a car or a pedestrian)

6 A call of "clear" at a junction = safe to proceed

7 A call of "easy" at any time = slow down and be prepared to stop

8 pointing a spread palm down to the road surface beside your leg on either side and "waving" at the road surface = uncertain surface on the road (e.g., gravel, oil, or broken glass)

fit skills—stretching

Getting into the habit of stretching after every ride will help you maintain flexibility (particularly important for muscles like the hip flexors, calves, and hamstrings, which cycling tends to tighten), and may even help you avoid certain types of injury. The stretches shown here can be built into a simple routine that should take no longer than 15 minutes to complete. Each stretch should be held without bouncing for 30 to 45 seconds, and make sure to stretch both legs (or arms) for each.

CALF STRETCH 1

Step one foot forward about three feet and bend that knee into a lunge. Keep the back leg straight and push the back heel down and back into the ground so that the foot stays flat.

CALF STRETCH 2

Step one foot forward about two feet and bend that knee into a lunge. Push the back heel down and back into the ground so that the foot stays flat, then lower the back knee toward the floor until you feel a stretch along the back of your calf and heel.

CLASS ACTS

If stretching alone is too much of a chore, you can always try yoga or Pilates classes. If you do, always look for a registered and qualified instructor and let them know how much cycling you've been doing.

HAMSTRING

Step forward about a foot with one leg. Straighten that leg, then bend the back knee slightly so that you "sit down" into that hip. Keeping your back straight, lean forward until you feel a stretch in the back of your leg, then raise your toes off the floor (keeping the heel grounded) to deepen the stretch.

QUADRICEPS

Stand with your feet and knees together. Stand on one leg and bend the other knee to bring your heel close to your bottom. Take hold of the top of the foot of the bent leg and pull the heel in towards your bottom as far as you can, then tip your pelvis up and forward until you feel a stretch along the front of your thigh.

fit skills—stretching

GLUTES

Lie on your back with your feet together. Bend one knee and pull it in toward the middle of your chest, using both hands to make the stretch nice and deep. Hold that position, then pull the still-bent knee across your body and down toward the floor beside your hip, as far as is comfortable, using your opposite hand (your hips should rotate toward the hand side when you do this) and hold that position, too.

CHEST

Interlace your fingers behind your back with your arms straight. Press your hands down and back until you feel a stretch across your shoulders and chest, keeping your fingers interlaced (and ideally your palms pressed together).

UPPER BACK

Interlace your fingers in front of you so that they are level with your arms straight and with your shoulders. Extend through your shoulders to push your hands as far in front of your chest as you can.

FORWARD BEND

Stand with your feet hip-width apart. Relax your arms, shoulders and neck. Let your chin drop to your chest, then roll your shoulders forward and down as you gradually curl forward down your spine, vertebra by vertebra. Once you've bent forward as far as you can, let your neck relax completely and simply hang there to let your lower back and hamstrings relax.

BENT OUT OF SHAPE

Be careful not to push each stretch beyond where you feel comfortable. Relax into the position and focus on "letting go" rather than forcing yourself.

LUNGE

Step one foot forward about three feet and bend that knee into a lunge. Lower the back knee down onto the floor so that both of your knees are bent at right angles. Step the heel of the front leg forward slightly (to where the toes were until a moment ago), then bend the knee to bring your hips forward and down toward the floor as far as you can. Keep your back straight throughout the stretch. (You may also find it more comfortable to place a towel between your kneecap and the floor when doing this stretch.)

fit skills—weight training

Cycling's low-impact nature makes it very easy on the joints and tendons, which means there's far less risk of injuries from overuse or pounding than in many other sports. Unfortunately, that very low-impact nature means that cycling alone is not always enough for maintenance and preservation of bone density. This is important, for as we age our muscles and bones become weaker, and our tendons become brittle. Cycling by itself will not typically provide the attention we need in this area, but thankfully a little focused gym-work can. Even better, regular gym training like this can also improve your fitness on the bike, helping you ride both further and faster.

RAISING QUESTIONS

What weights should I use?
All of the exercises here can be done with either dumbbells or a barbell. The preferred weight to use is mentioned in the description of the exercise.

Do I need to join a gym?
You could buy a decent set of weights from a sports shop and train at home, but it's usually better when starting out to train in a good gym with staff who can help you lift safely.

Should I use the same weight for everything?
Different exercises use different muscles, and some will be stronger than others so you'll need to use different weights for the different lifts.

How fast should I lift?
A good maxim is "drive up and lower slowly". Make the first part of the exercise where your muscles are really working fast and smooth, and then lower the weight slowly and deliberately.

How much rest should I take?
You shouldn't need to take a rest after each rep, but you should certainly take between 30 seconds and three minutes between sets, depending on how hard you're working.

REVERSE LUNGE
Stand with a dumbbell in each hand, your feet close together and your knees slightly bent. Keeping your hips facing forward and your back straight, step one foot back about one arm's length, bending the knee of the front leg as you do so. Lower the knee of the stepped back leg towards the ground, but before it touches, drive with your forward leg to step the rear leg up and forward so your feet are together again. Alternate legs until you have completed all the reps planned for both legs.

HOW OFTEN? HOW HEAVY?
You don't need to train a lot with weights—twice a week would probably do—but for the positive impact we're hoping for with your bones, you should before long be looking to do workouts with fewer repetitions using heavier weights, rather than lots of work with lighter ones that are easy for you. When you first start, spend a month perfecting the technique for the exercises shown and letting your body get used to the strains of gym work, then step up the effort.

Here's what you might do:

MONTH

1 3 x 10-12 reps of each exercise (use a light weight)

2 3 x 6-8 reps (use weights heavy enough that you have to really work to complete the last rep of each set)

3 4 x 6-8 reps (with the same weights as Month Two)

4 3 x 6-8 reps (but try using slightly heavier weights)

5 4 x 6-8 reps (with the same weights as Month Four)

You can keep repeating the Month Four/Month Five cycles as you get stronger, or simply settle at that point.

fit skills—weight training

BENCH PRESS

Lie back on a flat bench holding a barbell with a wider than shoulder-width overhand grip and your arms outstretched perpendicular to the floor. The bar should be above your chest. Keeping your lower back on the bench and your feet on the floor, slowly lower the bar until it just touches your chest, then exhale and press it back up until the arms are straight once more.

DEADLIFT

Pick up a barbell with a wider than shoulder-width overhand grip and stand, with your feet shoulder-width apart, so that the barbell is hanging in front of your thighs. Keeping your back straight and your arms hanging, inhale and slowly bend at the knees and squat down as if sitting into a chair until the backs of your thighs are parallel to the ground. Exhale as you look forward and push up with your legs, keeping your back straight.

CURL AND PRESS

Stand with your arms by your sides and a dumbbell in each hand. Keeping your elbows close to your sides and the rest of your body still, use your biceps to curl the weights up until your hands are in front of your shoulders, palms facing towards you. From here, bring your elbows away from your sides to rotate the weights until your palms are facing away from you, then smoothly press the dumbbells up above your head. Reverse the steps to lower the weights back down to begin the next rep.

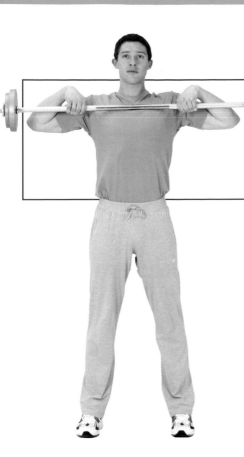

UPRIGHT ROW

Pick up a barbell with a wider than shoulder-width overhand grip and stand, with your feet shoulder-width apart, so that the barbell is hanging in front of your thighs. Keeping your back straight, exhale and pull the bar up towards your collarbone so that the bar stays close to your torso (your elbows will flare out to the sides as you do this). When you feel your shoulder and neck muscles squeeze, slowly lower the bar down and begin the next rep.

OVER/UNDER

In an overhand grip, when you look down at your hand you should see the back of your palm. With an underhand grip you should be able to see your fingers and thumb.

BENT-OVER ROW

Pick up a barbell with a wider than shoulder-width overhand grip and stand, with your feet shoulder-width apart, so that the barbell is hanging in front of your thighs. Bend your knees slightly and tip your torso forward (as if you are trying to use the barbell to touch your toes), keeping your back straight and your gaze slightly forward. Slowly lower the barbell towards the floor until your arms are straight. Exhale as you pull the barbell up towards the bottom of your ribcage, using your shoulders and back to lift. Squeeze your shoulder blades together, then lower the bar slowly until your arms are straight, and begin the next rep. Keep your upper body still and straight throughout.

fit skills—core training

The muscles of your stomach, lower back, and hips make up your "core." These are the muscles that hold you stable when you move. In fact, they fire before any other muscles to stabilize you and provide a steady platform for almost every movement you make. Unfortunately, pedaling along, bent over a bicycle, doesn't use these muscles evenly or completely—so here's a simple routine to even things out:

REVERSE SUPERMAN

Lie on your front with your arms stretched out above your head. Squeeze your right glute hard and bring your right leg up off the floor as far as you can without bending it. Holding the leg in place, raise your head and left arm off the floor slightly until you feel your lower back squeeze. Pause, then slowly lower both together and repeat with the left leg and right arm. Keep alternating as you do three sets of 10-20 reps.

PLANK

Lie on your front but propped up on your forearms. Squeeze your quads to lift you onto your toes, then squeeze your glutes together to level your hips and then pull your stomach in until your legs, hips, torso, and head are in a perfectly straight line. Hold this position for 15-60 seconds (you may shake a bit at first), then slowly lower back down. Repeat twice more.

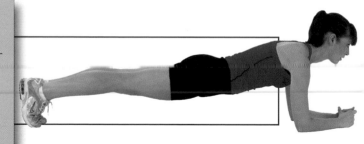

BRIDGE

Lie on your back with your knees bent to 90 degrees, your feet flat on the ground, and your arms down by your sides. Pull your stomach muscles in and squeeze your glutes together to lift your hips and lower and mid back off the floor until your thighs and chest are in line. Pause, then slowly lower to the start position. Do three sets of 10-20 reps, trying to raise your hips a little higher off the floor with each one.

SIDE PLANK

Lie on your right side but propped up on your right forearm and with your left arm flat against your side. Contract your quads, glutes, and abs, and raise your hips off the floor until your spine and legs form a perfectly straight line. Hold this position for 15-60 seconds, then gently lower your hip to the floor and switch sides. Keep your shoulders, chest, and hips at right angles to the floor at all times, and try not to stick your butt out!

CRUNCH

Lie on your back with your knees bent to 90 degrees and your feet flat on the ground. Cross your arms over your chest, relax your shoulders, and pull your stomach muscles in. Use your stomach muscles to lift your head, shoulders, and upper back off the floor. Keeping your stomach muscles pulled in, "crunch" the bottom of your ribcage down towards your pelvis as best you can, then slowly lower your back, shoulders, and head to the start position. Try not to tense your neck as you do three sets of 10-20 reps.

RAINBOWS

Lie on your back with your knees bent to 90 degrees, feet flat on the ground, and your arms stretched out to each side. Pull your stomach in and lift your feet up until your thighs are perpendicular to the floor and above your hips. Keep your shoulders and head flat on the floor, lower your knees to your right until the outside of that leg touches the floor (your waist will twist as you do this, and your left hip will naturally come off the floor). Without releasing your stomach, untwist so your legs come back to the middle and then twist so that they lower down to the left. Alternate right then left as you do three sets of 10-20 reps.

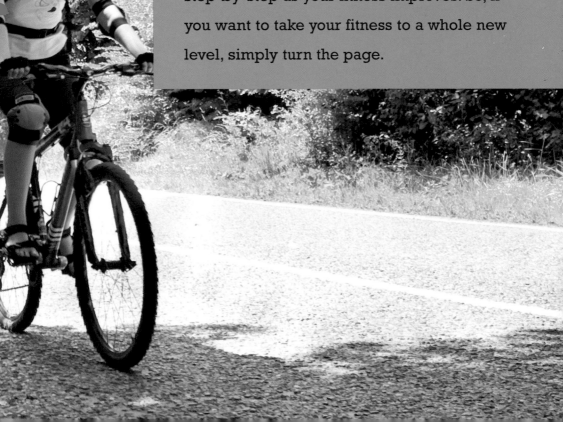

training programs

The best way to improve your fitness is to find a plan and stick to it. This last chapter contains six such plans, ranging in length from four to twelve weeks, and covering goals from simply starting to ride regularly to setting a time for 100 miles. All the plans are carefully designed to work as individual units or as a progression, building on each other step-by-step as your fitness improves. So, if you want to take your fitness to a whole new level, simply turn the page.

training—the basics

Over the next few pages you'll find a series of progressive training programs. If you're new to cycling, start at Level One and gradually work your way to whichever level you like at your own speed. If you're a rider already, have a flick through these pages, and then pick out the plan that looks right for you. Here's what each level involves:

MAXIMUM HEART RATE

Maximum Heart Rate
MEN = 214 – (0.8 x age)
WOMEN = 209 – (0.9 x age)

So, a 50-year-old-woman would have an approximate MHR of 164 beats per minute. (0.9 x 50 = 45, and 209 – 45 = 164)

LEVEL ONE

A basic program that includes four rides a week, gradually building up from 30 minutes to an hour over eight weeks.

LEVEL TWO

A slightly more challenging phase with four rides a week lasting an hour or more, the longest building up to 90 minutes in the course of four weeks.

LEVEL THREE

The first of the twelve-week programs gradually increases your Sunday ride duration to three hours while keeping the remaining three rides fairly constant.

FOLLOWING THE PLANS

All the rides in all the plans (with the exception of Levels Five and Six) are described in terms of time and effort. This means that you can follow them whether your top speed is 10 mph or 40 mph. The efforts are described in broad terms, or zones, based on how they should feel.

You'll find six effort zones mentioned in the plans: Easy, Endurance, Steady, Brisk, Hard, and Very Hard. Here's what each one relates to:

Effort	You feel you can...	Target Heart Rate	Exertion Level (1-10)
EASY	Chat, laugh, and even sing	below 65% MHR	5 or less
ENDURANCE	Still hold a conversation	65–75% MHR	5–6
STEADY	Speak in short sentences but no more	75–80% MHR	6–7
BRISK	Ride for an hour at most	80–85% MHR	8
HARD	Do nothing but pedal and breathe!	90–95% MHR	9
VERY HARD	Be happy it's over so soon!	Just go for it!	10!

The third column of the table contains a series of percentage ranges as target heart rates. This is the best way to monitor and refine your efforts when riding. Simply buy a heart rate monitor, calculate your approximate maximum heart rate (MHR) using the formulae on the opposite page, work out the percentages using your MHR figure as 100 percent, and then wear your heart rate monitor when you ride and stay within the boundaries for the effort zone that's given in the training program. Aim to start at the bottom of the zone and let the heart rate rise gradually up to (but not above) the upper limit.

LEVEL FOUR

A twelve-week program with slightly fewer hours per week (but still four rides) to allow you to focus on riding harder and increasing your speed.

LEVEL FIVE

A twelve-week program involving four or five rides a week and a gradual increase in distance to be covered as you build up to a crowning ride of 100 miles or 100 kilometres (62 miles), whichever you choose.

LEVEL SIX

A twelve-week program involving four or five rides a week, some high intensity efforts and weekend rides of up to six hours.

starting out

New to riding as a form of regular exercise? Then this is where you start. Your first month or so of riding should focus on building a habit for regular riding at a relatively easy, enjoyable pace. Don't worry too much about your speed or distance at this point, simply build up the time on the bike. If you've bought a heart rate monitor (and it's certainly a good idea) use it to guide your effort as you follow this program, staying in zones one and two (65-75% maximum heart rate) during all your rides. If you're not using a heart rate monitor keep your effort nice and steady—you should be able to cycle and still hold an easy conversation at the same time.

This first eight-week plan is designed to build up your riding safely and sensibly until you're able to ride four times a week for a whole hour without stopping.

ZERO TO HERO

One of the beauties of cycling is that, because it's a low-impact activity, you can build up the amount you do rather quickly, even if you're starting from scratch. Don't be alarmed if as you look over the training plan the rides seem to increase in length too quickly. You'll find you'll make quick progress.

Q&A – WHY EIGHT WEEKS?

For two reasons. First, it takes between six to eight weeks for most people's fitness to adapt to a new level of exercise. Second, eight weeks gives us roughly two month-long blocks, which means you can increase the amount of riding you're doing slowly and even have a little extra rest in week four to encourage your body to recover and adapt.

WEEK	MONDAY	TUESDAY	
1	30 minutes of easy riding. Stay on a flat quiet route.	Rest	
2	30 minutes of easy riding. Stay on a flat quiet route.	Rest	
3	40 minutes of easy riding. Stay on a flat quiet route.	Rest	
4	30 minutes of easy riding. Stay on a flat quiet route.	Rest	
5	40 minutes of easy riding. Stay on a flat quiet route.	Rest	
6	50 minutes of easy riding. Stay on a flat quiet route.	Rest	
7	50 minutes of easy riding. Stay on a flat quiet route.	Rest	
8	60 minutes of easy riding. Stay on a flat quiet route.	Rest	

WEDNESDAY	THURSDAY	FRIDAY	SATURDAY	SUNDAY
30 minutes of easy to steady riding. Stay on a flat quiet route.	Rest	30 minutes of easy to steady riding. Stay on a flat quiet route.	Rest	30 minutes of easy to steady riding. Stay on a flat quiet route.
40 minutes of easy to steady riding. Stay on a flat quiet route.	Rest	30 minutes of easy to steady riding. Stay on a flat quiet route.	Rest	40 minutes of easy to steady riding Stay on a flat quiet route.
40 minutes of easy to steady riding. Stay on a flat quiet route.	Rest	40 minutes of easy to steady riding. Stay on a flat quiet route.	Rest	40 minutes of easy to steady riding. Stay on a flat quiet route.
40 minutes of easy riding. Stay on a flat quiet route.	Rest	30 minutes of easy riding. Stay on a flat quiet route.	Rest	40 minutes of easy to steady riding. Stay on a flat quiet route.
50 minutes of easy to steady riding. Stay on a flat quiet route.	Rest	40 minutes of easy to steady riding. Stay on a flat quiet route.	Rest	50 minutes of easy to steady riding. Stay on a flat quiet route.
50 minutes of easy to steady riding. Stay on a flat quiet route.	Rest	50 minutes of easy to steady riding. Stay on a flat quiet route.	Rest	50 minutes of easy to steady riding. Stay on a flat quiet route.
60 minutes of easy to steady riding. Stay on a flat quiet route.	Rest	50 minutes of easy to steady riding. Stay on a flat quiet route.	Rest	60 minutes of easy to steady riding. Stay on a flat quiet route.
60 minutes of easy to steady riding. Stay on a flat quiet route.	Rest	60 minutes of easy to steady riding. Stay on a flat quiet route.	Rest	60 minutes of easy to steady riding. Stay on a flat quiet route.

2 riding for fitness

After a month or two getting into the swing of regular riding, you'll be surprised how comfortable you feel on the bike. You could simply stick with what you're doing and simply enjoy the process of riding for an hour. But to really improve your fitness,

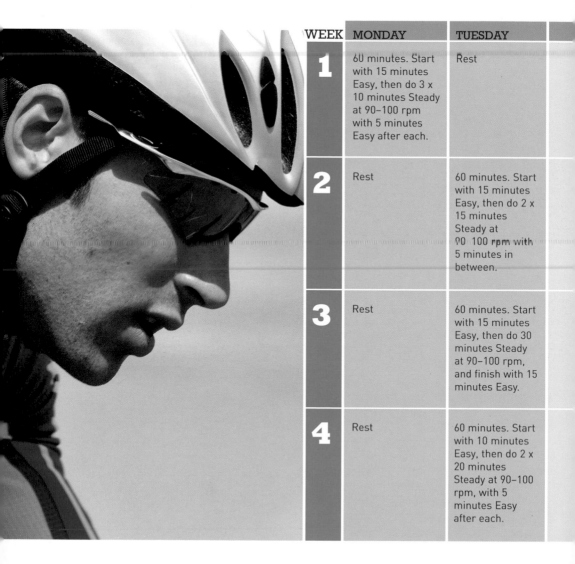

WEEK	MONDAY	TUESDAY	
1	60 minutes. Start with 15 minutes Easy, then do 3 x 10 minutes Steady at 90–100 rpm with 5 minutes Easy after each.	Rest	
2	Rest	60 minutes. Start with 15 minutes Easy, then do 2 x 15 minutes Steady at 90–100 rpm with 5 minutes in between.	
3	Rest	60 minutes. Start with 15 minutes Easy, then do 30 minutes Steady at 90–100 rpm, and finish with 15 minutes Easy.	
4	Rest	60 minutes. Start with 10 minutes Easy, then do 2 x 20 minutes Steady at 90–100 rpm, with 5 minutes Easy after each.	

it's better to mix things up. The program below is designed to improve your basic aerobic and cardiovascular fitness by gradually introducing some blocks of different intensities of riding. Each week, the Sunday ride gets a little longer and the amount of quicker riding increases until the fourth week, which is designed to be repeated again and again until you feel ready for a new challenge.

Q&A – WHY DO DIFFERENT RIDES?

Mixing your riding up over the course of a week gives you the opportunity to work on different riding skills and to develop your overall fitness from different directions. It's also much easier to motivate yourself when each ride is different; simply repeating the same route over and over again soon becomes dull.

WEDNESDAY	THURSDAY	FRIDAY	SATURDAY	SUNDAY
60 minutes Endurance effort on a hilly route. Use your gears to maintain 90–95 rpm.	Rest	Rest	60 minutes. Start with 30 minutes Easy, then pick up the pace and do 30 minutes at Endurance effort.	60 minutes Endurance effort on a flat or gently rolling route.
Rest	60 minutes Endurance effort on a hilly route. Use your gears to maintain 90–95 rpm.	Rest	60 minutes. Start with 30 minutes Easy, then do 20 minutes Endurance, then 10 minutes Steady.	70 minutes Endurance effort on a flat or gently rolling route.
Rest	60 minutes Endurance effort on a hilly route. Use your gears to maintain 90–95 rpm.	Rest	60 minutes. Start with 25 minutes Easy, then do 20 minutes Endurance, then 15 minutes Steady.	80 minutes Endurance effort on a flat or gently rolling route.
Rest	60 minutes Endurance effort on a hilly route. Use your gears to maintain 90–95 rpm.	Rest	60 minutes. Start with 20 minutes Easy, then do 20 minutes Endurance, then 20 minutes Steady.	90 minutes Endurance effort on a flat or gently rolling route.

building a long ride

One of the great pleasures of cycling is that it gives you the ability to exercise continuously for a long time. The 12 week program that you'll find on these four pages assumes that you are already able to ride for 90 minutes without stopping once a week, and will build your endurance slowly but surely until you've doubled that to three hours on a bicycle. Sound nuts? It really isn't, as you'll discover.

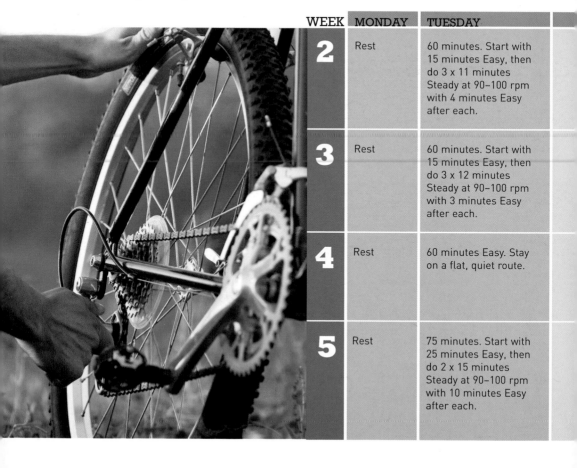

WEEK	MONDAY	TUESDAY	
1	60 minutes. Start with 15 minutes Easy, then do 3 x 10 minutes Steady at 90–100 rpm with 5 minutes Easy after each.	Rest	

WEEK	MONDAY	TUESDAY	
2	Rest	60 minutes. Start with 15 minutes Easy, then do 3 x 11 minutes Steady at 90–100 rpm with 4 minutes Easy after each.	
3	Rest	60 minutes. Start with 15 minutes Easy, then do 3 x 12 minutes Steady at 90–100 rpm with 3 minutes Easy after each.	
4	Rest	60 minutes Easy. Stay on a flat, quiet route.	
5	Rest	75 minutes. Start with 25 minutes Easy, then do 2 x 15 minutes Steady at 90–100 rpm with 10 minutes Easy after each.	

Q&A – WHY RIDE FOR SO LONG?

If you're looking to lose weight, relatively long, steady rides are best. Research suggests that efforts at around your first lactic threshold (which should feel no harder than 'steady') burn more fat in total than either harder or easier efforts. The longer you ride, the more your body will tend to turn to body fat for fuel, too.

TOP TIP

To stay fresh for your long rides on Sunday, don't let your effort rise too high on Saturday's ride. Stay below Steady on even the steepest climbs.

WEDNESDAY	THURSDAY	FRIDAY	SATURDAY	SUNDAY
60 minutes. Start with 30 minutes Easy, then do 20 minutes Endurance, then 10 minutes Steady.	Rest	Rest	60 minutes Endurance effort on a hilly route. Use your gears to maintain 90–100 rpm.	90 minutes Endurance effort on a flat or gently rolling route.

WEDNESDAY	THURSDAY	FRIDAY	SATURDAY	SUNDAY
Rest	60 minutes. Start with 30 minutes Easy, then do 20 minutes Endurance, then 10 minutes Steady.	Rest	60 minutes Endurance effort on a hilly route. Use your gears to maintain 90–100 rpm.	1 hour 45 minutes Endurance effort on a flat or gently rolling route.
Rest	60 minutes. Start with 30 minutes Easy, then do 20 minutes Endurance, then 10 minutes Steady.	Rest	60 minutes Endurance effort on a hilly route. Use your gears to maintain 90–100 rpm.	2 hours Endurance effort on a flat or gently rolling route.
Rest	60 minutes Endurance effort on a hilly route. Use your gears to maintain 90–100 rpm.	Rest	60 minutes Easy. Stay on a flat, quiet route.	90 minutes Endurance effort on a flat or gently rolling route.
Rest	60 minutes. Start with 25 minutes Easy, then do 20 minutes Endurance, then 15 minutes Steady.	Rest	60 minutes Endurance effort on a hilly route. Use your gears to maintain 90–100 rpm.	2 hours Endurance effort on a flat or gently rolling route.

3

building a long ride continued

PLEASURES OF A LONG RIDE

Long bike rides aren't simply about burning fat and building endurance; they're also a great way to explore. Here are a few ideas of ways to spice them up:

Finish at a local café, and treat yourself (sensibly!) at the end of the ride.

Ride out to friend's place for lunch and then have them drive you home later on.

Plan a route that takes you out into countryside or around a park.

Pack a picnic and stop to eat at the halfway point.

Enter and ride a charity cycling event.

TOP TIP

Weeks Four, Eight and 12 are deliberately easier to give your body time to adapt and recover. Take the opportunity to back off, even if you don't think you need it.

WEEK	MONDAY	TUESDAY	WEDNESDAY	
6	Rest	75 minutes. Start with 25 minutes Easy, then do 2 x 16 minutes Steady at 90–100 rpm with 9 minutes Easy after each.	Rest	
7	Rest	75 minutes. Start with 25 minutes Easy, then do 2 x 17 minutes Steady at 90–100 rpm with 8 minutes Easy after each.	Rest	
8	Rest	60 minutes Easy. Stay on a flat, quiet route.	Rest	
9	Rest	75 minutes. Start with 15 minutes Easy, then do 2 x 18 minutes Steady at 90–100 rpm with 14 minutes Easy in between. Finish with 10 minutes Easy.	Rest	
10	Rest	75 minutes. Start with 15 minutes Easy, then do 2 x 19 minutes Steady at 90–100 rpm with 12 minutes Easy in between. Finish with 10 minutes Easy.	Rest	
11	Rest	75 minutes. Start with 15 minutes Easy, then do 2 x 20 minutes Steady at 90–100 rpm with 10 minutes Easy in between. Finish with 10 minutes Easy.	Rest	
12	Rest	60 mins Easy. Stay on a flat, quiet route.	Rest	

THURSDAY	FRIDAY	SATURDAY	SUNDAY
60 minutes. Start with 25 minutes Easy, then do 20 minutes Endurance, then 15 minutes Steady.	Rest	60 minutes Endurance effort on a hilly route. Use your gears to maintain 90–100 rpm.	2 hours 15 minutes Endurance effort on a flat or gently rolling route.
60 minutes. Start with 25 minutes Easy, then do 20 minutes Endurance, then 15 minutes Steady.	Rest	75 minutes Endurance effort on a hilly route. Use your gears to maintain 90 100 rpm.	2 hours 30 minutes Endurance effort on a flat or gently rolling route.
60 minutes Endurance effort on a hilly route. Use your gears to maintain 90–100 rpm.	Rest	75 minutes Easy. Stay on a flat, quiet route.	90 minutes Endurance effort on a flat or gently rolling route.
60 minutes. Start with 20 minutes Easy, then do 20 minutes Endurance, then 20 minutes Steady.	Rest	75 minutes Endurance effort on a hilly route. Use your gears to maintain 90–100 rpm.	2 hours 30 minutes Endurance effort on a flat or gently rolling route.
60 minutes. Start with 20 minutes Easy, then do 20 minutes Endurance, then 20 minutes Steady.	Rest	75 minutes Endurance effort on a hilly route. Use your gears to maintain 90–100 rpm.	2 hours 45 minutes Endurance effort on a flat or gently rolling route.
60 minutes. Start with 20 minutes Easy, then do 20 minutes Endurance, then 20 minutes Steady.	Rest	75 minutes Endurance effort on a hilly route. Use your gears to maintain 90–100 rpm.	3 hours Endurance effort on a flat or gently rolling route.
60 mins. Endurance effort on a hilly route. Use your gears to maintain a cadence of 90-100 rpm.	Rest	60 mins Easy. Stay on a flat, quiet route.	3 hours Endurance effort on a flat or gently rolling route.

increasing your speed

Regular long rides will help you lose weight and keep you fit, but after a while your improvements will probably start to level off. When this happens, perhaps the best thing to do is change your focus. This 12 week program switches from improving your endurance to improving your speed. Fair warning: the riding will be harder than in levels One to Three, but we've also reduced the amount you'll be doing each week, so it should be an even trade off.

Q&A—HOW HARD SHOULD I WORK?

Gauging your effort is one of the hardest cycling skills to develop. If you're using a heart rate monitor, you can use the training zones on pages 74 and 75, but if not, brisk riding should feel "comfortably hard" (you should be breathing deeply but not panting, and you should be able to speak in short sentences). Hard efforts are a little more difficult to pin down. You're aiming for "eight or nine out of 10" in terms of how hard you think you could ever push, but as a general rule, make the efforts in Week One a little easier than you think you could really manage, and try to sustain that speed as the efforts get a little longer each week.

TOP TIP

Hold back for the first five minutes of your "test" rides in Weeks Four, Eight and 12, and try to lift the pace at five minutes, and again at 10. Don't simply hammer and hope!

WEEK	MONDAY	TUESDAY	
1	60 minutes. Start with 15 minutes Easy, then do 5 minutes Steady, then another 5 minutes Easy. Do 10 x 1 minute Hard at 95–105 rpm with 1 minute Easy after each. Finish with 15 minutes Easy.	Rest	

WEEK	MONDAY	TUESDAY	
2	Rest	60 minutes. Start with 11 minutes Easy, then do 5 minutes Steady, then another 5 minutes Easy. Do 6 x 2 minutes Hard at 95–105 rpm with 2 minutes Easy after each. Finish with 15 minutes Easy.	
3	Rest	60 minutes. Start with 10 minutes Easy, then do 5 minutes Steady, then another 5 minutes Easy. Do 5 x 3 minutes Hard at 95–105 rpm with 3 minutes Easy after each. Finish with 10 minutes Easy.	
4	Rest	60 minutes Easy. Stay on a flat, quiet route.	

WEDNESDAY	THURSDAY	FRIDAY	SATURDAY	SUNDAY
60 minutes. Start with 30 minutes Easy, then do 20 minutes Brisk, then 10 minutes Easy.	Rest	Rest	90 minutes Endurance effort on a hilly route. Use your gears to maintain 100–110 rpm.	2 hours Endurance effort on a flat or gently rolling route.

WEDNESDAY	THURSDAY	FRIDAY	SATURDAY	SUNDAY
Rest	60 minutes. Start with 28 minutes Easy, then do 22 minutes Brisk, then 10 minutes Easy.	Rest	90 minutes Endurance effort on a hilly route. Use your gears to maintain 100–110 rpm.	2 hours Endurance effort on a flat or gently rolling route. Ride Brisk up any hills in the last 30 minutes.
Rest	60 minutes. Start with 26 minutes Easy, then do 24 minutes Brisk, then 10 minutes Easy.	Rest	90 minutes Endurance effort on a hilly route. Use your gears to maintain 100–110 rpm.	2 hours Endurance effort on a flat or gently rolling route. Ride Brisk up any hills in the last 60 minutes.
Rest	60 minutes Endurance effort on a hilly route. Use your gears to maintain 90–100 rpm.	Rest	60 minutes Easy. Stay on a flat, quiet route.	90 minutes. Map yourself a 5–10 mile "test" route, ride it once Easy to warm up, then time how long it takes you to ride it fast. Ride it Easy again to cool down, then head home.

4

increasing your speed continued

TOP TIP

Don't fall into the trap of thinking that riding hard and "big gear" are the same thing. Stick to the cadence targets given, and for all your other riding try to stay above 85 rpm.

WEEK	MONDAY	TUESDAY	
5	Rest	60 minutes. Start with 10 minutes Easy, then do 5 minutes Steady, then another 5 minutes Easy. Do 5 x 3 minutes Hard at 95–105 rpm with 3 minutes Easy after each. Finish with 10 minutes Easy.	
6	Rest	60 minutes. Start with 10 minutes Easy, then do 5 minutes Steady, then another 5 minutes Easy. Do 4 x 4 minutes Hard at 95–105 rpm with 4 minutes Easy after each. Finish with 8 minutes Easy.	
7	Rest	60 minutes. Start with 5 minutes Easy, then do 5 minutes Steady, then another 5 minutes Easy. Do 4 x 5 minutes Hard at 95–105 rpm with 5 minutes Easy after each. Finish with 5 minutes Easy.	
8	Rest	60 minutes Easy. Stay on a flat, quiet route.	

WEDNESDAY	THURSDAY	FRIDAY	SATURDAY	SUNDAY
Rest	60 minutes. Start with 28 minutes Easy, then do 22 minutes Brisk, then 10 minutes Easy.	Rest	90 minutes Endurance effort on a hilly route. Use your gears to maintain 100–110 rpm.	2 hours Endurance effort on a flat or gently rolling route. Ride Brisk up any hills in the last 30 minutes.
Rest	60 minutes. Start with 26 minutes Easy, then do 24 minutes Brisk, then 10 minutes Easy.	Rest	90 minutes Endurance effort on a hilly route. Use your gears to maintain 100–110 rpm.	2 hours Endurance effort on a flat or gently rolling route. Ride Brisk up any hills in the last 60 minutes.
Rest	60 minutes. Start with 24 minutes Easy, then do 26 minutes Brisk, then 10 minutes Easy.	Rest	90 minutes Endurance effort on a hilly route. Use your gears to maintain 100–110 rpm.	2 hours Endurance effort on a flat or gently rolling route. Ride Brisk up any hills in the last 75 minutes.
Rest	60 minutes. Endurance effort on a hilly route. Use your gears to maintain 90–100 rpm.	Rest	60 minutes Easy. Stay on a flat, quiet route.	90 minutes. Head out to your "test" route again. Ride it three times, just like last time, but try to beat your time from Week Four when you do the fast lap!

increasing your speed continued

WEATHER OR NOT?

Don't fall into the trap of forcing yourself out for a hard ride in bad conditions. Heavy rain, fog, ice, and extreme heat are not safe riding conditions when you're pushing yourself. Simply reschedule things for a better day.

WEEK	MONDAY	TUESDAY	
9	Rest	60 minutes. Start with 5 minutes Easy, then do 5 minutes Steady, then another 5 minutes Easy. Do 4 x 5 minutes Hard at 95–105 rpm with 5 minutes Easy after each. Finish with 5 minutes Easy.	
10	Rest	60 minutes. Start with 9 minutes Easy, then do 5 minutes Steady, then another 5 minutes Easy. Do 4 x 5 minutes Hard at 95–105 rpm with 4 minutes Easy after each. Finish with 5 minutes Easy.	
11	Rest	60 minutes. Start with 10 minutes Easy, then do 5 minutes Steady, then another 5 minutes Easy. Do 4 x 5 minutes Hard at 95–105 rpm with 3 minutes Easy after each. Finish with 8 minutes Easy.	
12	Rest	60 minutes Easy. Stay on a flat, quiet route.	

WEDNESDAY	THURSDAY	FRIDAY	SATURDAY	SUNDAY
Rest	60 minutes. Start with 26 minutes Easy, then do 24 minutes Brisk, then 10 minutes Easy.	Rest	90 minutes Endurance effort on a hilly route. Use your gears to maintain 100–110 rpm.	2 hours Endurance effort on a flat or gently rolling route. Ride Brisk up any hills in the last 60 minutes.
Rest	60 minutes. Start with 24 minutes Easy, then do 26 minutes Brisk, then 10 minutes Easy.	Rest	90 minutes Endurance effort on a hilly route. Use your gears to maintain 100–110 rpm.	2 hours Endurance effort on a flat or gently rolling route. Ride Brisk up any hills in the last 75 minutes.
Rest	60 minutes. Start with 22 minutes Easy, then do 28 minutes Brisk, then 10 minutes Easy.	Rest	90 minutes Endurance effort on a hilly route. Use your gears to maintain 100–110 rpm.	2 hours Endurance effort on a flat or gently rolling route. Ride Brisk up any hills in the last 90 minutes.
Rest	60 minutes Endurance effort on a hilly route. Use your gears to maintain 90–100 rpm.	Rest	60 minutes Easy. Stay on a flat, quiet route.	90 minutes. One more try for a faster time on your "test" route again. Can you better the time from Week Eight?

your first challenge ride

If you leaf back through the previous few pages of programs you'll notice that they all work toward a goal: riding for an hour, building a long weekend ride, and improving your speed over a set distance. Outcome goals like these are central to sticking to an exercise plan because they give purpose to what you're doing—and having a purpose helps sustain your interest. So, what do you do when you've achieved those goals? You could just settle back and simply maintain your newfound fitness, but if you fancy taking your cycling a step further, a challenge ride is the next logical step. This 12 week plan shows you how to prepare for your first challenge.

Q&A – WHAT'S A CHALLENGE RIDE?

A challenge ride is anything you like, really. It's your goal. This particular plan builds up riding distance with the aim of riding a "century," (100 miles or kilometers), but whether you do that alone, with friends, in a charity ride, or adapt the program so that it prepares you for a cross-country bicycle tour spanning several days or even more or even a long mountain bike event is up to you.

A WORD ON DISTANCE

The Sunday rides in this plan are unusual in that they are set in distance rather than time because they work you toward a century ride. Whether you choose to train in miles and work toward a full 100-mile ride or follow the slightly easier alternative and train in kilometers for a metric century is up to you. Just remember which unit you've decided to use and stick with it throughout the program.

WEEK	MONDAY	TUESDAY	
1	60 minutes Endurance effort.	60 minutes Easy or Rest.	

WEEK	MONDAY	TUESDAY	
2	Rest	60 minutes Endurance effort.	
3	Rest	60 minutes Endurance effort.	
4	Rest	60 minutes Easy on a quiet, flat route.	
5	Rest	60 minutes as 30 minutes Endurance, then 30 minutes Steady.	

TOP TIP

Try to make the terrain you cover on your Sunday distance rides as similar as possible to the terrain you'll be riding on in Week 12's target challenge ride.

WEDNESDAY	THURSDAY	FRIDAY	SATURDAY	SUNDAY
Rest	60 minutes Endurance effort. Choose a rolling route, but keep your cadence at 95–105 rpm.	Rest	90 minutes Endurance on a flat route including 3 x 10 minutess at 110 rpm.	40 miles or kilometers Endurance.

WEDNESDAY	THURSDAY	FRIDAY	SATURDAY	SUNDAY
60 minutes Easy or Rest.	60 minutes Endurance effort. Choose a rolling route, but keep your cadence at 95–105 rpm.	Rest	90 minutes Endurance on a flat route including 3 x 12 minutes at 110 rpm.	50 miles or kilometers Endurance.
60 minutes Easy or Rest.	60 minutes Endurance effort. Choose a rolling route, but keep your cadence at 95–105 rpm.	Rest	90 minutes Endurance on a flat route including 3 x 15 minutes at 110 rpm.	60 miles or kilometers Endurance.
Rest	60 minutes Easy on a quiet, flat route.	60 minutes Easy on a quiet, flat route.	Rest	3 hours Easy on a flat to rolling route.
60 minutes Easy or Rest.	75 minutes Endurance effort. Choose a rolling route, but keep your cadence at 95–105 rpm.	Rest	90 minutes Endurance on a flat route including 3 x 10 minutes Steady at 90–100 rpm.	55 miles or kilometers Endurance.

5 your first challenge ride continued

TOP TIP

If you're planning a mountain-bike challenge ride, it may be easier to build up your Sunday distance on the road (at least in part). Still, do at least one ride a week off-road to sharpen your trail skills. Thursday's ride is probably best.

TOP TIP

Make sure you load up your energy supplies before your challenge ride in Week 12. Aim to eat about 5g of carbohydrate per pound of bodyweight—spaced out into lots of small meals and snacks—on the day before the ride.

WEEK	MONDAY	TUESDAY	WEDNESDAY
6	Rest	60 minutes as 20 minutes Endurance, then 40 minutes Steady.	60 minutes Easy or Rest.
7	Rest	60 minutes, with 15 minutes Endurance, then 45 minutes Steady.	60 minutes Easy or Rest.
8	Rest	60 minutes Easy on a quiet, flat route.	Rest
9	Rest	60 minutes including 3 x 10 minutes Brisk at 90–95 rpm with 5 minutes Easy after each.	60 minutes Easy or Rest.
10	Rest	60 minutes including 2 x 15 minutes Brisk at 90–95 rpm with 5 minutes Easy after each.	60 minutes Easy or Rest.
11	Rest	60 minutes including 30 minutes Brisk at 90–95 rpm in the middle.	60 minutes Easy or Rest.
12	Rest	Rest	60 minutes Easy.

TOP TIP

Make sure you're taking enough fuel with you on your rides, and make sure that what you use on your Sunday rides is the same as what you'll use in your challenge in Week 12.

THURSDAY	FRIDAY	SATURDAY	SUNDAY
75 minutes Endurance effort. Choose a rolling route, but keep your cadence at 95–105 rpm.	Rest	90 minutes Endurance on a flat route including 2 x 15 minutes Steady at 90–100 rpm.	65 miles or kilometers Endurance.
75 minutes Endurance effort. Choose a rolling route, but keep your cadence at 95–105 rpm.	Rest	90 minutes Endurance on a flat route including 2 x 20 minutes Steady at 90–100 rpm.	75 miles or kilometers Endurance.
60 minutes Easy on a quiet, flat route.	90 minutes Easy on a quiet, flat route.	Rest	3 hours Easy on a flat to rolling route.
90 minutes Endurance effort. Choose a rolling route, but keep your cadence at 95–105 rpm.	Rest	90 minutes Endurance on a flat route including 2 x 20 minutes Steady at 90–100 rpm.	70 miles or kilometers Endurance.
90 minutes Endurance effort. Choose a rolling route, but keep your cadence at 95–105 rpm.	Rest	90 minutes Endurance on a flat route including 2 x 25 minutes Steady at a cadence of 90-100 rpm.	80 miles or kilometers Endurance.
90 minutes Endurance effort. Choose a rolling route, but keep your cadence at 95–105 rpm.	Rest	90 minutes Endurance on a flat route including 2 x 30 minutes Steady at 90–100 rpm.	90 miles or kilometers Endurance.
Rest	60 minutes Easy.	Rest	50 miles or kilometers.

6 challenge performance 2

Once you've completed your first "challenge" event, you'll likely find that there's a nagging voice at the back of your head whispering to you that, with a little work, you could have done that faster, or continued to ride even farther. If you decide to listen to that little voice, here's an advanced training program that'll help you build to a new and higher level of riding.

Q&A – ISN'T THIS ALL A BIT SERIOUS?

That's up to you. If you want to improve at something the second time around (or even the third, fourth, or fifth), you'll probably have to accept that you'll need to work a little bit more because the goal has become more challenging. You don't have to push your limits to enjoy your cycling, but equally pushing those limits can be very fulfilling when you get it right. Above all, whatever you do, enjoy it.

TOP TIP

Be careful not to push too hard during your uphills on Sundays. Use a small gear, keep the effort down, and stay in the saddle to climb.

WEEK	MONDAY	TUESDAY	
1	90 minutes Endurance including 3 x 10 minutes Steady at 95–10 rpm with 5 minutes Easy after each.	60 minutes Easy or Rest.	
2	Rest	90 minutes Endurance including 2 x 15 minutes Steady at 95–10 rpm with 5 minutes Easy in between.	
3	Rest	90 minutes Endurance including 30 minutes Steady at 95–10 rpm in the middle.	
4	Rest	60 minutes Easy on a quiet, flat route.	
5	Rest	90 minutes Endurance including 3 x 10 minutes Brisk with 5–10 minutes Easy after each.	

WEDNESDAY	THURSDAY	FRIDAY	SATURDAY	SUNDAY
Rest	90 minutes as 60 minutes Endurance, then 30 minutes Steady at 95–105 rpm.	Rest	2 hours, with 15 minutes Easy, then 90 minutes Steady at 95–105 rpm, then 15 minutes Easy. Stay on a flat route.	3 hours Endurance riding on a rolling route. Ride Brisk up any hills.
60 minutes Easy or Rest.	90 minutes, with 45 minutes Endurance, then 45 minutes Steady at 95–105 rpm.	Rest	2 hours, with 15 minutes Easy, then 90 minutes Steady at 95–105 rpm, then 15 minutes Easy. Stay on a flat route.	3 hours 30 minutes Endurance riding on a rolling route. Ride Brisk up any hills.
60 minutes Easy or Rest.	90 minutes, with 30 minutes Endurance, then 60 minutes Steady at 95–105 rpm.	Rest	2 hours, with 15 minutes Easy, then 90 minutes Steady at 95–105 rpm, then 15 minutes Easy. Stay on a flat route.	4 hours Endurance riding on a rolling route. Ride Brisk up any hills.
Rest	60 minutes Easy on a quiet, flat route but including 3 x 1 minute Hard and 3 x 30 seconds Hard.	Rest	60 minutes Easy on a quiet, flat route.	60 miles or kilometers over challenge-ride like terrain. Try to achieve the same average pace you hope to see in Week 12.
60 minutes Easy or Rest.	90 minutes, with 20 minutes Endurance, then 70 minutes Steady at 95–105 rpm.	Rest	2 hours, with 15 minutes Easy, then 90 minutes Steady at 95–105 rpm, then 15 minutes Easy. Stay on a flat route.	4 hours 30 minutes Endurance riding on a rolling route. Ride Brisk up any hills.

challenge performance 2 continued

TOP TIP

Ideally, do the Brisk blocks in Weeks Five to Seven up a long, gradual hill.

TOP TIP

Look carefully at the course of your chosen challenge. Plan when you can afford to take it easy and eat a little more (perhaps on a downhill), and know how hard you can safely push on any hills. It may even be worth heading out there in Weeks Four and Eight to ride parts of the route.

WEEK	MONDAY	TUESDAY	WEDNESDAY	
6	Rest	90 minutes Endurance including 3 x 12 minutes Brisk with 5–10 minutes Easy after each.	60 minutes Easy or Rest.	
7	Rest	90 minutes Endurance including 3 x 15 minutes Brisk with 5–10 minutes Easy after each.	60 minutes Easy or Rest.	
8	Rest	60 minutes Easy on a quiet, flat route.	Rest	
9	Rest	90 minutes Endurance including 2 x 20 minutes Brisk with 5 minutes Easy after each.	60 minutes Easy or Rest.	
10	Rest	90 minutes Endurance including 2 x 20 minutes Brisk with 5 minutes Easy after each.	60 minutes Easy or Rest.	
11	Rest	90 minutes Endurance including 2 x 20 minutes Brisk with 5 minutes Easy after each.	Rest	
12	Rest	60 minutes Easy on a quiet, flat route but including 3 x 1 minute Hard and 3 x 30 seconds Hard.	Rest	

TOP TIP

You'll notice that Week 11 contains considerably less riding than Week 10. This is to give you more time to rest and recover before your big day in Week 12.

THURSDAY	FRIDAY	SATURDAY	SUNDAY
90 minutes, with 10 minutes Endurance, then 80 minutes Steady at 95–105 rpm.	Rest	2 hours, with 15 minutes Easy, then 90 minutes Steady at 95–105 rpm, then 15 minutes Easy. Stay on a flat route.	5 hours Endurance riding on a rolling route. Ride Brisk up any hills.
90 minutes Steady at 95–105 rpm.	Rest	2 hours, with 15 minutes Easy, then 90 minutes Steady at 95–105 rpm, then 15 minutes Easy. Stay on a flat route.	5 hours 30 minutes Endurance riding on a rolling route. Ride Brisk up any hills.
90 minutes, with 45 minutes Endurance, 30 minutes Steady, 15 minutes Brisk. Stay on a flat, quiet route.	Rest	2 hours on a rolling route as 15 minutes Easy, then 90 minutes Steady at 95–105 rpm, then 15 minutes Easy.	5 hours 30 minutes Endurance riding on a rolling route. Ride Brisk up any hills.
90 minutes as 45 minutes Endurance, 30 minutes Steady, 15 minutes Brisk. Stay on a flat, quiet route.	Rest	2 hrs on a rolling route as 15 minutes Easy, then 90 minutes Steady at a cadence of 95-105 rpm, then 15 minutes Easy	5 hours 30 minutes Endurance riding on a rolling route. Ride Brisk up any hills.
90 minutes, with 40 minutes Endurance, 30 minutes Steady, 20 minutes Brisk. Stay on a flat, quiet route.	Rest	2 hours on a rolling route, with 15 minutes Easy, then 90 minutes Steady at 95–105 rpm, then 15 minutes Easy.	6 hours Endurance riding on a rolling route. Ride Brisk up any hills.
90 minutes, with 35 minutes Endurance, 30 minutes Steady, 25 minutes Brisk. Stay on a flat, quiet route.	Rest	90 minutes on a rolling route, with 15 minutes Easy, then 60 minutes Steady, then 15 minutes Easy.	3 hours Endurance riding on challenge-ride like terrain.
60 minutes Easy on a quiet, flat route but including 3 x 1 minute Hard and 3 x 30 seconds Hard.	Rest	60 minutes Easy on a quiet, flat route.	Challenge ride!

how to change a flat

Sooner or later every tire goes flat. Sharp rocks, shards of glass, bits of metal, and simple time can cause slits and splits in the rubber of your tires. It's not "if" but "when"—an eventual certainty that you will get a flat. Here's what to do about it:

YOU WILL NEED...

A spare inner tube
Three strong, plastic tire levers
A small high-pressure pump or
CO_2 canister tire inflator

1 Remove the wheel from the bike, then turn the bike upside down to rest on the saddle and handlebars to prevent the chain from getting dirty. If it's your back wheel that has the puncture, remember to first shift to your smallest cog at the back and your smallest chain-ring at the front. This makes it easier to get the wheel on and off around the chain.

2 Release all the air from the tire if it hasn't gone down completely, then insert all three of your tire levers between the rim of the wheel and the sidewall of the tire so that they hook underneath the bead, or edge of the tire, where it meets the rim. The levers should be side by side and about three inches apart. It's easiest if this is done as far away from the tire valve as possible.

3 Pull down on all the levers at once so that they pivot on the rim and point towards the center of the wheel. This action will lift the tire bead out of the rim.

4 Take the right-most lever in your hand and gradually run it around the rim, levering the rest of that side of the tire off the rim. Do not release both sides of the tire from the rim.

5 Pull out the damaged inner tube and look along it to see where in relation to the valve the puncture is, then run your fingers carefully around the inside of the tire looking for anything sharp like wire or glass that may have poked through. Pay particular attention to the area around where you think the puncture happened and fish out any debris that may remain lodged in the tire.

6 When you're sure that the tire is free of any foreign objects and that the inner surface of the tire and rim are clear, very slightly inflate your replacement inner tube and push it into the tire. Start by inserting the valve into the rim and then gently roll the inner tube up into the tire all the way around.

PATCHING THINGS UP

It's far quicker to carry a spare inner tube with you when you ride and simply replace the flat one when you're out riding than to try patching the hole by the side of the road. You certainly can repair inner tubes and reuse them, but it is best done in the comfort of your home or garage.

7 Using your thumbs, hook the bead of the tire back into the rim, starting near the valve and working slowly around both sides of the wheel at once. You may have to release some air from the inner tube and use your tire levers to flip the last part of the bead into place.

8 Release all the rest of the air from valve of the new inner tube. It should be completely inside the tire at this point. Carefully observe the tire and rim all the way around the wheel to make sure that there are no sections of new inner tube getting pinched between the bead of the tire and the rim.

9 Pump up your tire, then reinsert the wheel into the frame, making sure that you replace the chain on the correct cog as needed and that you replace the wheel properly so you can continue riding safely. This may seem like a long process, but with practice you'll find it only takes a couple of minutes to do.

how to clean your bike

Quite apart from looking nice, a clean bike will last longer, work better, and go faster than a dirty bike. If you're riding regularly it's worth setting aside a little time to clean your bike, oil your chain and gears, and pump up your tires. Here's a step by step guide to cleaning a dirty bike:

YOU WILL NEED...

A soft, dry brush
Two sponges and some water
A smooth, sturdy cloth
A box chain cleaner

A gentle solvent
Some concentrated bike degreaser
 (get this from a good bike shop)
Some WD40 or other light spray oil
Some chain lube

1 Starting at the underside of your saddle, work down your bike from top to bottom, using the brush to remove any clumps and lumps of dried dirt and dust. Remember to brush the undersides of your brakes, the insides of your seat and chain stays, and the underside of your forks. (It may be easier to do these areas by quickly taking the wheel out for easy access.)

2 Once the bike is clear of dried dirt, use one sponge and some water to wipe the whole thing down, working from top to bottom. Remember to sponge down the tires and rims as well as the frame.

3 Using one side of the cloth, wipe down the chain by spinning the pedals backwards with your hand (if the chain jams, lift the back wheel off the floor and spin the pedals forward until the chain slips back into line).

4 Fill the box chain cleaner with the concentrated degreaser and attach it to the chain as directed and spin the pedals backwards as directed to clean the chain.

5 Remove the box chain cleaner, and use the other sponge and some clean water to rinse the chain and gears thoroughly. Wipe down the cassette and chain-rings, lift the back wheel off the floor, and spin the pedals forward a few times to force the remaining water out, then leave it to dry.

6 While the chain is drying use the solvent and the other side of your cloth to polish any remaining dirt or smears from your frame, brakes, and even the spokes of your wheels. In a pinch, Windex or another alcohol-based cleaner will work for this.

7 When the chain is dry, spray it with WD40 to force the water out of the links, wipe it down again with the cloth and then carefully oil it with your proper chain lube.

8 When you go riding again, enjoy your clean and smoothly-functioning bike!

Cleaning your bike is not a job for the living room. Do it in your driveway or outside.

PRESSURE GAUGE

Your tires should have a recommended level of inflation (in PSI) on the side. Make sure they're pumped to that pressure—ideally before every ride you do. Under-filled tires are susceptible to "pinch flats"—so called because you hit something in the road like a pot-hole with an edge that pinches your tube against your rim and makes a distinctive puncture mark that looks like a snake bite. You can also easily damage your rim in these instances. Plus, it's harder to ride on an under-filled tire. Think about trying to bounce a mostly-flat basketball—same concept. And over-filled tires are prone to blow-outs, usually in the sidewall. It will not be possible to repair these tubes.

cycling diary

Keeping a record of your cycle rides can be instrumental in helping you discover how to improve on your fitness levels. You will be able to see at a glance when you rode your best, what the conditions were, what you ate and drank before and during your ride, and you will be able to monitor your progress through the schedules as you get fitter, healthier, and stronger.

WEEK 1

DATE

OBJECTIVES

_____

_____

_____

MONDAY

RIDE

1

TIME/DISTANCE	COMMENTS

2

TIME/DISTANCE	COMMENTS

EFFORT

1

TIME/DISTANCE		

2

TIME/DISTANCE	REPS	RECOVERY

3

TIME/DISTANCE	REPS	RECOVERY

WEATHER CONDITIONS

1

2

HOW DO YOU FEEL

BEFORE THE RIDE

AFTER THE RIDE

TUESDAY

RIDE

1

TIME/DISTANCE	COMMENTS

2

TIME/DISTANCE	COMMENTS

EFFORT

1

TIME/DISTANCE	REPS	RECOVERY

2

TIME/DISTANCE	REPS	RECOVERY

3

TIME/DISTANCE	REPS	RECOVERY

WEATHER CONDITIONS

1

2

HOW DO YOU FEEL

BEFORE THE RIDE

AFTER THE RIDE

WEDNESDAY

RIDE

1

TIME/DISTANCE	COMMENTS

2

TIME/DISTANCE	COMMENTS

EFFORT

1

TIME/DISTANCE	REPS	RECOVERY

2

TIME/DISTANCE	REPS	RECOVERY

3

TIME/DISTANCE	REPS	RECOVERY

WEATHER CONDITIONS

1

2

HOW DO YOU FEEL

BEFORE THE RIDE

AFTER THE RIDE

THURSDAY

RIDE

1

TIME/DISTANCE	COMMENTS

2

TIME/DISTANCE	COMMENTS

EFFORT

1

TIME/DISTANCE	REPS	RECOVERY

2

TIME/DISTANCE	REPS	RECOVERY

3

TIME/DISTANCE	REPS	RECOVERY

WEATHER CONDITIONS

1

2

HOW DO YOU FEEL

BEFORE THE RIDE

AFTER THE RIDE

comments

If you need to wear a jacket in the cooler weather to keep warm, make sure that you choose a tight fitting one. A loose jacket can act like a drogue parachute, slowing you down and making you expend more energy.

Are you drinking enough?

Remember to drink before, during, and after a ride. Aim to drink a pint of water (roughly half a liter) half an hour before you train. On long rides, take one small cup of liquid for every 15-20 minutes of cycling.

comments

FRIDAY

RIDE

1

TIME/DISTANCE	COMMENTS

2

TIME/DISTANCE	COMMENTS

EFFORT

1

TIME/DISTANCE	REPS	RECOVERY

2

TIME/DISTANCE	REPS	RECOVERY

3

TIME/DISTANCE	REPS	RECOVERY

WEATHER CONDITIONS

1

2

HOW DO YOU FEEL
BEFORE THE RIDE

AFTER THE RIDE

SATURDAY

RIDE

1

TIME/DISTANCE	COMMENTS

2

TIME/DISTANCE	COMMENTS

EFFORT

1

TIME/DISTANCE	REPS	RECOVERY

2

TIME/DISTANCE	REPS	RECOVERY

3

TIME/DISTANCE	REPS	RECOVERY

WEATHER CONDITIONS

1

2

HOW DO YOU FEEL
BEFORE THE RIDE

AFTER THE RIDE

SUNDAY

RIDE

1

TIME/DISTANCE	COMMENTS

2

TIME/DISTANCE	COMMENTS

EFFORT

1

TIME/DISTANCE	REPS	RECOVERY

2

TIME/DISTANCE	REPS	RECOVERY

3

TIME/DISTANCE	REPS	RECOVERY

WEATHER CONDITIONS

1

2

HOW DO YOU FEEL

BEFORE THE RIDE

AFTER THE RIDE

comments

DATE

GOALS MET	
GOALS EXCEEDED	
NEXT WEEK	

RIDING NOTES

EFFORT NOTES

REFUELING NOTES

WEEK 2

OBJECTIVES

_____
_____
_____

DATE

MONDAY

RIDE

1

TIME/DISTANCE	COMMENTS

2

TIME/DISTANCE	COMMENTS

EFFORT

1

TIME/DISTANCE		

2

TIME/DISTANCE	REPS	RECOVERY

3

TIME/DISTANCE	REPS	RECOVERY

WEATHER CONDITIONS

1

2

HOW DO YOU FEEL

BEFORE THE RIDE

AFTER THE RIDE

TUESDAY

RIDE

1

TIME/DISTANCE	COMMENTS

2

TIME/DISTANCE	COMMENTS

EFFORT

1

TIME/DISTANCE	REPS	RECOVERY

2

TIME/DISTANCE	REPS	RECOVERY

3

TIME/DISTANCE	REPS	RECOVERY

WEATHER CONDITIONS

1

2

HOW DO YOU FEEL

BEFORE THE RIDE

AFTER THE RIDE

WEDNESDAY

RIDE

1

TIME/DISTANCE	COMMENTS

2

TIME/DISTANCE	COMMENTS

EFFORT

1

TIME/DISTANCE	REPS	RECOVERY

2

TIME/DISTANCE	REPS	RECOVERY

3

TIME/DISTANCE	REPS	RECOVERY

WEATHER CONDITIONS

1

2

HOW DO YOU FEEL

BEFORE THE RIDE

AFTER THE RIDE

THURSDAY

RIDE

1

TIME/DISTANCE	COMMENTS

2

TIME/DISTANCE	COMMENTS

EFFORT

1

TIME/DISTANCE	REPS	RECOVERY

2

TIME/DISTANCE	REPS	RECOVERY

3

TIME/DISTANCE	REPS	RECOVERY

WEATHER CONDITIONS

1

2

HOW DO YOU FEEL

BEFORE THE RIDE

AFTER THE RIDE

comments

Although you develop more power while standing on the pedals, on longer hill climbs, stay seated and spin at 80-85 RPM. This helps you to burn less energy and use your bigger gluteal (butt) and hip muscles to your advantage.

Smooth gears

The secret to smooth shifting, especially on hills, lies in planning. Anticipate you'll need an easier gear and shift a few seconds ahead of time—including shifting to an easier gear at the bottom of the hill while you still have momentum.

comments

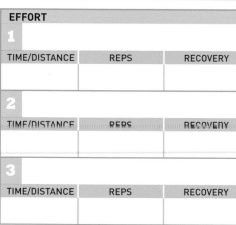

FRIDAY

RIDE

1

TIME/DISTANCE	COMMENTS

2

TIME/DISTANCE	COMMENTS

EFFORT

1

TIME/DISTANCE	REPS	RECOVERY

2

TIME/DISTANCE	REPS	RECOVERY

3

TIME/DISTANCE	REPS	RECOVERY

WEATHER CONDITIONS

1

2

HOW DO YOU FEEL

BEFORE THE RIDE

AFTER THE RIDE

SATURDAY

RIDE

1

TIME/DISTANCE	COMMENTS

2

TIME/DISTANCE	COMMENTS

EFFORT

1

TIME/DISTANCE	REPS	RECOVERY

2

TIME/DISTANCE	REPS	RECOVERY

3

TIME/DISTANCE	REPS	RECOVERY

WEATHER CONDITIONS

1

2

HOW DO YOU FEEL

BEFORE THE RIDE

AFTER THE RIDE

SUNDAY

RIDE

1

TIME/DISTANCE	COMMENTS

2

TIME/DISTANCE	COMMENTS

EFFORT

1

TIME/DISTANCE	REPS	RECOVERY

2

TIME/DISTANCE	REPS	RECOVERY

3

TIME/DISTANCE	REPS	RECOVERY

WEATHER CONDITIONS

1

2

HOW DO YOU FEEL

BEFORE THE RIDE

AFTER THE RIDE

comments

DATE

GOALS MET

GOALS EXCEEDED

NEXT WEEK

RIDING NOTES

EFFORT NOTES

REFUELING NOTES

WEEK 3

DATE

OBJECTIVES

_____

_____

_____

MONDAY

RIDE

1

TIME/DISTANCE	COMMENTS

2

TIME/DISTANCE	COMMENTS

EFFORT

1

TIME/DISTANCE		

2

TIME/DISTANCE	REPS	RECOVERY

3

TIME/DISTANCE	REPS	RECOVERY

WEATHER CONDITIONS

1

2

HOW DO YOU FEEL
BEFORE THE RIDE

AFTER THE RIDE

TUESDAY

RIDE

1

TIME/DISTANCE	COMMENTS

2

TIME/DISTANCE	COMMENTS

EFFORT

1

TIME/DISTANCE	REPS	RECOVERY

2

TIME/DISTANCE	REPS	RECOVERY

3

TIME/DISTANCE	REPS	RECOVERY

WEATHER CONDITIONS

1

2

HOW DO YOU FEEL
BEFORE THE RIDE

AFTER THE RIDE

WEDNESDAY

RIDE

1

TIME/DISTANCE	COMMENTS

2

TIME/DISTANCE	COMMENTS

EFFORT

1

TIME/DISTANCE	REPS	RECOVERY

2

TIME/DISTANCE	REPS	RECOVERY

3

TIME/DISTANCE	REPS	RECOVERY

WEATHER CONDITIONS

1

2

HOW DO YOU FEEL

BEFORE THE RIDE

AFTER THE RIDE

THURSDAY

RIDE

1

TIME/DISTANCE	COMMENTS

2

TIME/DISTANCE	COMMENTS

EFFORT

1

TIME/DISTANCE	REPS	RECOVERY

2

TIME/DISTANCE	REPS	RECOVERY

3

TIME/DISTANCE	REPS	RECOVERY

WEATHER CONDITIONS

1

2

HOW DO YOU FEEL

BEFORE THE RIDE

AFTER THE RIDE

comments

Be careful of wet metal when riding in the rain—manhole covers, grates, and metal bridge surfaces become like ice when they are wet. Slow down when approaching them and try to cross at a right angle, keeping your bike as upright as possible.

Body language

When training it is important to listen to your body. If you ignore these signals then it can easily lead to over training which can do more harm than good. A day of rest can be just as beneficial as a hard day of riding!

comments

FRIDAY

RIDE

1

TIME/DISTANCE	COMMENTS

2

TIME/DISTANCE	COMMENTS

EFFORT

1

TIME/DISTANCE	REPS	RECOVERY

2

TIME/DISTANCE	REPS	RECOVERY

3

TIME/DISTANCE	REPS	RECOVERY

WEATHER CONDITIONS

1

2

HOW DO YOU FEEL
BEFORE THE RIDE

AFTER THE RIDE

SATURDAY

RIDE

1

TIME/DISTANCE	COMMENTS

2

TIME/DISTANCE	COMMENTS

EFFORT

1

TIME/DISTANCE	REPS	RECOVERY

2

TIME/DISTANCE	REPS	RECOVERY

3

TIME/DISTANCE	REPS	RECOVERY

WEATHER CONDITIONS

1

2

HOW DO YOU FEEL
BEFORE THE RIDE

AFTER THE RIDE

SUNDAY

RIDE

1

TIME/DISTANCE	COMMENTS

2

TIME/DISTANCE	COMMENTS

EFFORT

1

TIME/DISTANCE	REPS	RECOVERY

2

TIME/DISTANCE	REPS	RECOVERY

3

TIME/DISTANCE	REPS	RECOVERY

WEATHER CONDITIONS

1

2

HOW DO YOU FEEL

BEFORE THE RIDE

AFTER THE RIDE

comments

DATE

GOALS MET

GOALS EXCEEDED

NEXT WEEK

RIDING NOTES

EFFORT NOTES

REFUELING NOTES

WEEK 4

DATE

OBJECTIVES

MONDAY

RIDE

1

TIME/DISTANCE	COMMENTS

2

TIME/DISTANCE	COMMENTS

EFFORT

1

TIME/DISTANCE		

2

TIME/DISTANCE	REPS	RECOVERY

3

TIME/DISTANCE	REPS	RECOVERY

WEATHER CONDITIONS

1

2

HOW DO YOU FEEL
BEFORE THE RIDE

AFTER THE RIDE

TUESDAY

RIDE

1

TIME/DISTANCE	COMMENTS

2

TIME/DISTANCE	COMMENTS

EFFORT

1

TIME/DISTANCE	REPS	RECOVERY

2

TIME/DISTANCE	REPS	RECOVERY

3

TIME/DISTANCE	REPS	RECOVERY

WEATHER CONDITIONS

1

2

HOW DO YOU FEEL
BEFORE THE RIDE

AFTER THE RIDE

WEDNESDAY

RIDE

1

TIME/DISTANCE	COMMENTS

2

TIME/DISTANCE	COMMENTS

EFFORT

1

TIME/DISTANCE	REPS	RECOVERY

2

TIME/DISTANCE	REPS	RECOVERY

3

TIME/DISTANCE	REPS	RECOVERY

WEATHER CONDITIONS

1

2

HOW DO YOU FEEL

BEFORE THE RIDE

AFTER THE RIDE

THURSDAY

RIDE

1

TIME/DISTANCE	COMMENTS

2

TIME/DISTANCE	COMMENTS

EFFORT

1

TIME/DISTANCE	REPS	RECOVERY

2

TIME/DISTANCE	REPS	RECOVERY

3

TIME/DISTANCE	REPS	RECOVERY

WEATHER CONDITIONS

1

2

HOW DO YOU FEEL

BEFORE THE RIDE

AFTER THE RIDE

comments

A cycling buddy can help keep you motivated. Try to choose someone who has similar goals as you, and arrange a mutually convenient schedule that you know you will both be able to stick to. Review your goals and schedule regularly.

Keep it different

Repeating the same kind of training day in and day out can take the pleasure out of your rides. If commuting is part of your cycle routine, try different routes and different speeds to keep it fun.

comments

FRIDAY

RIDE

1

TIME/DISTANCE	COMMENTS

2

TIME/DISTANCE	COMMENTS

EFFORT

1

TIME/DISTANCE	REPS	RECOVERY

2

TIME/DISTANCE	REPS	RECOVERY

3

TIME/DISTANCE	REPS	RECOVERY

WEATHER CONDITIONS

1

2

HOW DO YOU FEEL

BEFORE THE RIDE

AFTER THE RIDE

SATURDAY

RIDE

1

TIME/DISTANCE	COMMENTS

2

TIME/DISTANCE	COMMENTS

EFFORT

1

TIME/DISTANCE	REPS	RECOVERY

2

TIME/DISTANCE	REPS	RECOVERY

3

TIME/DISTANCE	REPS	RECOVERY

WEATHER CONDITIONS

1

2

HOW DO YOU FEEL

BEFORE THE RIDE

AFTER THE RIDE

SUNDAY

RIDE

1

TIME/DISTANCE	COMMENTS

2

TIME/DISTANCE	COMMENTS

EFFORT

1

TIME/DISTANCE	REPS	RECOVERY

2

TIME/DISTANCE	REPS	RECOVERY

3

TIME/DISTANCE	REPS	RECOVERY

WEATHER CONDITIONS

1

2

HOW DO YOU FEEL

BEFORE THE RIDE

AFTER THE RIDE

comments

DATE

GOALS MET

GOALS EXCEEDED

NEXT WEEK

RIDING NOTES

EFFORT NOTES

REFUELING NOTES

WEEK 5

DATE

OBJECTIVES

MONDAY

RIDE

1

TIME/DISTANCE	COMMENTS

2

TIME/DISTANCE	COMMENTS

EFFORT

1

TIME/DISTANCE		

2

TIME/DISTANCE	REPS	RECOVERY

3

TIME/DISTANCE	REPS	RECOVERY

WEATHER CONDITIONS

1

2

HOW DO YOU FEEL

BEFORE THE RIDE

AFTER THE RIDE

TUESDAY

RIDE

1

TIME/DISTANCE	COMMENTS

2

TIME/DISTANCE	COMMENTS

EFFORT

1

TIME/DISTANCE	REPS	RECOVERY

2

TIME/DISTANCE	REPS	RECOVERY

3

TIME/DISTANCE	REPS	RECOVERY

WEATHER CONDITIONS

1

2

HOW DO YOU FEEL

BEFORE THE RIDE

AFTER THE RIDE

WEDNESDAY

RIDE

1

TIME/DISTANCE	COMMENTS

2

TIME/DISTANCE	COMMENTS

EFFORT

1

TIME/DISTANCE	REPS	RECOVERY

2

TIME/DISTANCE	REPS	RECOVERY

3

TIME/DISTANCE	REPS	RECOVERY

WEATHER CONDITIONS

1

2

HOW DO YOU FEEL

BEFORE THE RIDE

AFTER THE RIDE

THURSDAY

RIDE

1

TIME/DISTANCE	COMMENTS

2

TIME/DISTANCE	COMMENTS

EFFORT

1

TIME/DISTANCE	REPS	RECOVERY

2

TIME/DISTANCE	REPS	RECOVERY

3

TIME/DISTANCE	REPS	RECOVERY

WEATHER CONDITIONS

1

2

HOW DO YOU FEEL

BEFORE THE RIDE

AFTER THE RIDE

comments

On rides of over an hour you will need something to help boost your energy levels. Ready prepared energy bars or gels work very well, but can be expensive. Alternatively you could take a banana, a flapjack, or some dried fruit, such as prunes.

Go clipless

They can be tricky to get used to, but clipless pedals really can improve your cycling. They allow you to push down evenly for a larger part of the pedaling cycle. There is also a small element of "pulling up" on the pedal at the back of the stroke.

comments

FRIDAY

RIDE

1

TIME/DISTANCE	COMMENTS

2

TIME/DISTANCE	COMMENTS

EFFORT

1

TIME/DISTANCE	REPS	RECOVERY

2

TIME/DISTANCE	REPS	RECOVERY

3

TIME/DISTANCE	REPS	RECOVERY

WEATHER CONDITIONS

1

2

HOW DO YOU FEEL
BEFORE THE RIDE

AFTER THE RIDE

SATURDAY

RIDE

1

TIME/DISTANCE	COMMENTS

2

TIME/DISTANCE	COMMENTS

EFFORT

1

TIME/DISTANCE	REPS	RECOVERY

2

TIME/DISTANCE	REPS	RECOVERY

3

TIME/DISTANCE	REPS	RECOVERY

WEATHER CONDITIONS

1

2

HOW DO YOU FEEL
BEFORE THE RIDE

AFTER THE RIDE

SUNDAY

RIDE

1

TIME/DISTANCE	COMMENTS

2

TIME/DISTANCE	COMMENTS

EFFORT

1

TIME/DISTANCE	REPS	RECOVERY

2

TIME/DISTANCE	REPS	RECOVERY

3

TIME/DISTANCE	REPS	RECOVERY

WEATHER CONDITIONS

1

2

HOW DO YOU FEEL

BEFORE THE RIDE

AFTER THE RIDE

comments

DATE

GOALS MET	
GOALS EXCEEDED	
NEXT WEEK	

RIDING NOTES

EFFORT NOTES

REFUELING NOTES

WEEK 6

DATE

OBJECTIVES

MONDAY

RIDE

1

TIME/DISTANCE	COMMENTS

2

TIME/DISTANCE	COMMENTS

EFFORT

1

TIME/DISTANCE		

2

TIME/DISTANCE	REPS	RECOVERY

3

TIME/DISTANCE	REPS	RECOVERY

WEATHER CONDITIONS

1

2

HOW DO YOU FEEL

BEFORE THE RIDE

AFTER THE RIDE

TUESDAY

RIDE

1

TIME/DISTANCE	COMMENTS

2

TIME/DISTANCE	COMMENTS

EFFORT

1

TIME/DISTANCE	REPS	RECOVERY

2

TIME/DISTANCE	REPS	RECOVERY

3

TIME/DISTANCE	REPS	RECOVERY

WEATHER CONDITIONS

1

2

HOW DO YOU FEEL

BEFORE THE RIDE

AFTER THE RIDE

WEDNESDAY

RIDE

1

TIME/DISTANCE	COMMENTS

2

TIME/DISTANCE	COMMENTS

EFFORT

1

TIME/DISTANCE	REPS	RECOVERY

2

TIME/DISTANCE	REPS	RECOVERY

3

TIME/DISTANCE	REPS	RECOVERY

WEATHER CONDITIONS

1

2

HOW DO YOU FEEL

BEFORE THE RIDE

AFTER THE RIDE

THURSDAY

RIDE

1

TIME/DISTANCE	COMMENTS

2

TIME/DISTANCE	COMMENTS

EFFORT

1

TIME/DISTANCE	REPS	RECOVERY

2

TIME/DISTANCE	REPS	RECOVERY

3

TIME/DISTANCE	REPS	RECOVERY

WEATHER CONDITIONS

1

2

HOW DO YOU FEEL

BEFORE THE RIDE

AFTER THE RIDE

comments

Each day you use your bike, give it a quick check—particularly, the condition of the tires and their pressure. Every week, lubricate exposed moving parts, such as the chain and gear mechanisms, and check the wheel rims and brake blocks.

Don't spend too much

It is not necessary to spend a fortune to get a good quality bike. Look for a model from a manufacturer that also makes top end bicycles. Some of that technology will filter down into their mid to low price range models as well.

comments

FRIDAY

RIDE

1

TIME/DISTANCE	COMMENTS

2

TIME/DISTANCE	COMMENTS

EFFORT

1

TIME/DISTANCE	REPS	RECOVERY

2

TIME/DISTANCE	REPS	RECOVERY

3

TIME/DISTANCE	REPS	RECOVERY

WEATHER CONDITIONS

1

2

HOW DO YOU FEEL
BEFORE THE RIDE

AFTER THE RIDE

SATURDAY

RIDE

1

TIME/DISTANCE	COMMENTS

2

TIME/DISTANCE	COMMENTS

EFFORT

1

TIME/DISTANCE	REPS	RECOVERY

2

TIME/DISTANCE	REPS	RECOVERY

3

TIME/DISTANCE	REPS	RECOVERY

WEATHER CONDITIONS

1

2

HOW DO YOU FEEL
BEFORE THE RIDE

AFTER THE RIDE

SUNDAY

RIDE

1

TIME/DISTANCE	COMMENTS

2

TIME/DISTANCE	COMMENTS

EFFORT

1

TIME/DISTANCE	REPS	RECOVERY

2

TIME/DISTANCE	REPS	RECOVERY

3

TIME/DISTANCE	REPS	RECOVERY

WEATHER CONDITIONS

1

2

HOW DO YOU FEEL

BEFORE THE RIDE

AFTER THE RIDE

comments

DATE

GOALS MET

GOALS EXCEEDED

NEXT WEEK

RIDING NOTES

EFFORT NOTES

REFUELING NOTES

Glossary

aerobic: exercise at an intensity that allows the body's need for oxygen to be continually met. This intensity can be sustained for long periods.

aerodynamic: a design of cycling equipment or a riding position that reduces wind resistance; aero for short.

anaerobic: exercise above the intensity at which the body's need for oxygen can be met. This intensity can be sustained only briefly.

apex: the sharpest part of a turn where the transition from entering to exiting takes place.

bead: in tires, the edge along each side's inner circumference that fits into the rim.

blood glucose: a sugar, glucose is the only fuel that can be used by the brain.

blow up: to suddenly be unable to continue at the required pace due to overexertion.

bonk: a state of severe exhaustion caused mainly by the depletion of glycogen in the muscles because the rider has failed to eat or drink enough. Once it occurs, rest and high-carbohydrate foods are necessary for recovery.

boot: a small piece of material used inside a tire to cover a cut in the tread or sidewall. Without it, the tube will push through and blow out.

bpm: abbreviation for beats per minute in reference to heart rate.

bunch: the main cluster of riders in a race. Also called the group, pack, field or peloton.

cadence: the number of times during one minute that a pedal stroke is completed.

carve: Making a hard turn while maintaining a clean line. It can also mean to spin a bicycles rear tire and make a rut in the dirt.

century: a 100-mile ride.

chasers: those who are trying to catch a group or a lead rider.

circuit training: a weight training technique in which you move rapidly from exercise to exercise without rest.

cleat: a metal or plastic fitting on the sole of a cycling shoe that engages the pedal.

crosstraining: combining sports for mental refreshment and physical conditioning, especially during cycling's off-season.

downshift: to shift to a lower gear, i.e. a larger cog or smaller chainring.

drafting: riding closely behind another rider to take advantage of the windbreak (slipstream) and use about 20 percent less energy.

drivetrain: the components directly involved with making the rear wheel turn, i.e. the chain, crankset and cassette. Also called the power train.

granny gear: the lowest gear ratio, combining the small chainring with the largest cassette cog. It's mainly used for very steep cliffs. Named after the gear that grandmothers use most frequently.

hybrid: a bike that combines features of road and mountain bikes. Also called a cross bike.

intervals: a structured method of training that alternates brief, hard efforts with short periods of easier riding for partial recovery.

lactic acid: a substance formed during anaerobic metabolism when there is incomplete breakdown of glucose. It rapidly produces muscle fatigue and pain. Also called lactate.

LSD: long, steady distance. A training technique that requires a firm aerobic pace for at least two hours.

metric century: a 100-kilometer ride (62 miles).

overgear: using a gear ratio too big for the terrain or level of fitness.

overtraining: deep-seated fatigue, both physical and mental, caused by training at an intensity or volume too great for adaptation.

peak: a relatively short period during which maximum performance is achieved.

presta: the narrow European-style valve found on some inner tubes. A small metal cap on its end must be unscrewed before air can enter or exit.

psi: abbreviation for pounds per square inch. The unit of measure for tire inflation and air pressure in some suspensions.

RAAM: the Race Across America, contested from the west coast to the east every year since 1982.

reach: the combined length of a bike's top tube and stem, which determines the rider's distance to the handlebar.

resistance trainer: a stationary training device into which the bike is clamped. Pedaling resistance increases with pedaling speed to simulate actual riding. Also known as an indoor, wind, fluid, or mag trainer.

Schrader: an inner tube valve identical to those found on car tires. A tiny plunger in the center of its opening must be depressed for air to enter or exit.

slingshot: to ride up behind another rider with help from his draft, then use the momentum to sprint past.

slipstream: the pocket of calmer air behind a moving rider. Also called the draft.

soft-pedal: to rotate the pedals without actually applying power.

speedwork: a general term for intervals and other high-velocity training, such as sprints and time trials.

stage race: a multi-day event consisting of various types of races. The winner is the rider with the lowest elapsed time for all races (stages).

tempo: fast riding at a brisk cadence.

time trial (TT): a race against the clock in which individual riders start at set intervals and cannot give or receive a draft.

tubular: a lightweight tire that has its tube sewn inside the casing. Also called a sew-up. The tire is glued to the rim.

USA Cycling: the umbrella organization for American bicycle racing.

upshift: to shift to a higher gear, i.e. a smaller cog or larger chainring.

USCF: U.S. Cycling Federation, the organization that governs amateur road, cyclocross, and track racing in America. A division of USA Cycling.

velodrome: an oval banked track for bicycle racing.

wheelsucker: someone who drafts behind others but doesn't take a pull.

wind up: steady acceleration to an all-out effor

index

ACKNOWLEDGMENTS

Special thanks to Mike Cotty at Cannondale (www.cannondale.com) for his help with equipment and images.

Every effort has been made to credit everybody that appears in this book, and we apologize in advance for any unintentional omissions. We would be pleased to insert the appropriate acknowledgment in any subsequent edition of this publication.